SUPERVISION:

The ASTD Trainer's Sourcebook

Books in The ASTD Trainer's Sourcebook Series

SUPERVISION:

The ASTD Trainer's Sourcebook

Bobette Hayes Williamson

McGraw-Hill

New York San Francisco Washington D.C. Auckland Bogotá
Caracas Lisbon London Madrid Mexico City Milan
Montreal New Delhi San Juan Singapore
Sydney Tokyo Toronto

Library of Congress Catalog Card Number: 95-076446

McGraw-Hill

A Division of The McGraw-Hill Companies

1 2 3 4 5 6 7 8 9   MAL/MAL   9 0 0 9 8 7 6 5

ISBN: 0-07-053437-3

Sourcebook Team:

Co-Publishers:	Philip Ruppel, Training McGraw-Hill
	Nancy Olson, American Society for Training and Development
Acquisitions Editor:	Richard Narramore, Training McGraw-Hill
Editing Supervisor:	Paul R. Sobel, McGraw-Hill Professional Book Group
Production Supervisor:	Donald F. Schmidt, McGraw-Hill Professional Book Group
Series Advisor:	Richard L. Roe
Editing/Imagesetting:	Claire Condra Arias, Stacy Marquardt
	Ellipsys International Publications, Inc.

 This book is printed on recycled, acid-free paper containing a minimum of 50% recycled de-inked fiber.

Contents

Preface

I'd like to tell you how this series came about. As a long-time editor and resource person at University Associates/Pfeiffer & Company, I was frequently asked by trainers, facilitators, consultants, and instructors to provide them with training designs on a variety of topics. These customers wanted one-hour, half-day, and full-day programs on such topics as team-building, coaching, diversity, supervision, and sales. Along with the training designs, they required facilitator notes, participant handouts, flipchart ideas, games, activities, structured experiences, overhead transparencies, and instruments. But, that wasn't all. They wanted to be able to reproduce, customize, and adapt these materials to their particular needs—at no cost!

Later, as an independent editor, I shared these needs with Nancy Olson, the publisher at the American Society for Training and Development. Nancy mentioned that ASTD received many similar calls from facilitators who were looking for a basic library of reproducible training materials. Many of the classic training volumes, such as Jones and Pfeiffer's *Handbook of Structured Experiences* and Newstrom and Scannell's *Games Trainers Play* provided a variety of useful activities. However, they lacked training designs, handouts, overheads, and instruments—and, most importantly, they tended to be organized by method rather than by topic. You can guess the rest of the story: Welcome to *The ASTD Trainer's Sourcebook*.

This sourcebook is part of an open-ended series that covers the training topics most often found in many organizations. Instead of locking you into a prescribed "workbook mentality," this sourcebook will free you from having to buy more workbooks each time you present training. This volume contains everything you need—background information on the topic, facilitator notes, training designs, participant handouts, activities, instruments, flipcharts, overheads, and resources—and it's all reproducible! We welcome you to adapt it to your particular needs. Please photocopy. . . edit. . . add your name. . . add your client's name. Please don't tell us. . . it isn't necessary! Enjoy.

Richard L. Roe
ASTD Sourcebook Series Advisor

SUPERVISION:

The ASTD Trainer's Sourcebook

Chapter One:

Introduction

Welcome to *SUPERVISION: The ASTD Trainer's Sourcebook*—your one-stop reference for supervisory training materials. This complete resource package allows you to train new and experienced supervisors who work in a variety of settings: traditional Industrial Age enterprises, networked Information Age enterprises, or organizations that are in transition from bureaucratic to networked structures.

> ### SUPERVISION:
> ### THE ASTD TRAINER'S SOURCEBOOK
>
> This chapter describes the contents and structure of the book. It also shows you how to navigate through the book, and select the building blocks needed to create your own training program. Major topics are:
>
> - Sourcebook Organization.
>
> - Workshop Building Blocks.
>
> - Subject/Reference Matrix.
>
> - Time Block/Methods Matrix.
>
> - Navigating the Training Plans.
>
> - Understanding the Icons.
>
> - Formula for Supervision.

Sourcebook Organization

The sourcebook has ten chapters, an appendix, and an index.

1. Introduction

Chapter One explains how your sourcebook is organized. It also provides a *Subject/Reference Matrix* and a *Time Block/Methods Matrix* to help you navigate through the sourcebook and find just the right material for your workshop.

2. Background

Chapter Two provides the context for your supervision workshops. It discusses how and why supervision is changing as employers struggle to adapt to a fiercely competitive global economy. The chapter identifies four major segments of the new workforce, and provides specific techniques for managing workers from each segment. Finally, the chapter discusses how organizational structures are evolving from Industrial Age hierarchies to Information Age networks, and offers techniques for supervising in Information Age enterprises. The chapter also contains a glossary of key terms.

3. Workshop Preparation

Chapter Three gives general tips on workshop preparation, including how to design, administer, facilitate, conduct, and follow up on the training program. The chapter also has a workshop agenda template for blocking out the flow of your workshop, and a comprehensive checklist to help you remember the myriad of details associated with planning and delivering a workshop.

4. One-Day Supervision Workshop

Chapter Four offers a scripted training plan for a one-day workshop on "High-Performance Supervision." The workshop is designed for new supervisors and individuals considering supervision as a career. It also can serve as a refresher for experienced supervisors. The workshop includes skill-practice exercises and action planning to encourage participants to apply knowledge and skills gained during the workshop when they return to the job.

5. Half-Day Supervision Workshop

Turn to Chapter Five for a scripted half-day workshop on "Planning and Organizing Work." The purpose is to provide both new and experienced supervisors with background on and techniques for planning, organizing, and delegating. Skill practice and action planning encourage transfer of learning to the workplace.

6. One-Hour Supervision Workshop

This scripted one-hour workshop on "Communicating Instructions" provides new or experienced supervisors with techniques for giving instructions, as well as skill practice and observation. The workshop is ready to go "as is," or it can be customized to fit your needs.

7. Participant Handouts

Here are the masters from which you can create participant handouts, ready to be reproduced "as is," or customized to suit your needs. The handouts focus on the basics of supervision. They cover the four-step supervision process of planning, organizing, leading, and controlling; management levels; supervisory responsibilities and roles; and delegation.

8. Learning Activities

Chapter Eight is a collection of learning activities designed to create the high level of participant involvement that is key to the success of your sessions. Included are an icebreaker, discussion cases, skill-practice exercises, and demonstrations. Before each learning activity, you'll find instructions on its use.

9. Tools and Assessments

In this short collection of simple assessments, you'll find self-appraisals; surveys in which participants identify what planning, organizing, leading, and controlling tasks they perform; a skill-application planner to encourage transfer of learning to the workplace; and a sample workshop evaluation form. Before each assessment or tool, you'll find instructions on its use.

10. Overhead Transparencies

Photocopy these camera-ready masters on transparency film for professional-looking visuals to reinforce your presentations. The masters can be copied on plain paper for participant handouts. Also, the content can be hand-lettered on 2' x 3' flipchart paper.

11. Appendix: Recommended Resources

To learn more about supervision, refer to the books and periodicals cited in the selected bibliography. To locate training products, contact the providers mentioned under "Resources for Training Professionals."

Workshop Building Blocks

In this sourcebook, you have all the building blocks needed to create your own supervisory training programs. The following pages provide *Subject/Reference* and *Time Block/Methods* matrices to help you select the building blocks that fit your objectives.

Directions

To use the *Subject/Reference Matrix* on pages 5 through 7, follow the steps below:

1. To locate sourcebook material on a specific topic, go to Column A (Topic) and find the row that lists the topic needed. For example, if you want material on "Basic Supervision," go to Column A, Row 2 (Cell A-2).

2. Refer to the cells in the selected row to find page references for information and materials on the topic. For example, to locate learning activities on "Basic Supervision," go across Row 2 to the cell where the topic intersects with the "Learning Activities" column (Cell F-2).

3. Review the materials listed in Cell F-2, and select those that are appropriate for your group and time block.

4. Also, refer to the Appendix, *Recommended Resources*, for titles of videos/films that meet your requirements.

Subject/Reference Matrix

A. Topic	B. Background	C. Scripts	D. Handouts	E. Overheads	F. Learning Activities	G. Tools and Assessments	H. Reinforcement Session
1. Facilitation and Administration	pp. 4-12 pp. 33-52	One-Day Workshop, pp. 53-82 Half-Day Workshop, pp. 83-110 One-Hour Workshop, pp. 111-122		Round-Robin Skill-Practice, p. 223		Skill-Application Planning, pp. 208-210 Program Evaluation, pp. 211-212	Skill-Application Planning Option, pp. 208-210
2. Basics of Supervision	pp. 13-29	One-Day Workshop, modules 3 and 4, pp. 65-79	Basics of Supervision, p. 124 High-Performance Management versus Low-Octane Management, pp. 14-15 Management Levels, pp. 125-126 Supervisory Roles, p. 127 Supervisory Job Knowledge, p. 216 Management Skills, p. 217 Challenges Facing New Supervisors, p. 218	Management Process, p. 214 Management Levels, p. 215 Supervisory Responsibilities, p. 216 Supervisory Roles, p. 217 Supervisory Job Knowledge, p. 218 Management Skills, p. 219 Challenges Facing New Supervisors, p. 220	Get-Acquainted Treasure Hunt, pp. 136-137 He's Sinking Fast, pp.138-141 Delivering Unpopular News, pp. 142-145 Preserving the Friendship, pp. 146-148 Quality Is Below Standard, pp. 149-154 Ignoring the Chain of Command, pp. 155-159 Skill-Practice Observer Checklist, p. 154	Self-Appraisal, pp. 176-179 Supervisory Roles Assessment, pp. 180-185	Supervisory Roles Assessment Option, pp. 180-185

Subject/Reference Matrix

A. Topic	B. Background	C. Scripts	D. Handouts	E. Overheads	F. Learning Activities	G. Tools and Assessments	H. Reinforcement Session
3. Planning		Half-Day Workshop, Modules 1 and 2, pp. 90-99	Creating Goals and Objectives, p. 128; Implementing a Plan, p. 222	Implementing a Plan, p. 224	Going Through the Work Orders, pp. 160-164	Planning Survey, pp. 186-190; Workforce Trial Balance Planning, pp. 191-193	Workforce Trial Balance Planning, pp. 191-193
4. Organizing		Half-Day Workshop, Modules 3 and 4, pp. 100-110	Key Organizing Questions, p. 129		Going Through the Work Orders, pp. 160-167	Organizing Survey, pp. 194-197	
5. Delegating		Half-Day Workshop, Modules 1, 4, pp. 90-92, 103-110; One-Hour Workshop, pp. 111-122	What Is Delegation?, p. 130; The Delegation Process, p. 219; Giving Instructions, p. 220	Delegation Process, p. 221; Giving Instructions, p. 222	Ignoring the Chain of Command, pp. 155-159; Skill-Practice Observer Checklist, p. 149; Going Through the Work Orders, pp. 160-166; Delegation Planning and Skill Practice, pp. 167-169; Giving Instructions: Extra Mile Athletic Shoes, pp. 170-174		
6. Leading	pp. 14-25, 28-29	One-Day Workshop Module 5, pp. 65-74	Leading, p. 131; Leadership and Motivation, p. 132		Delivering Unpopular News, pp. 142-145	Leading Survey, pp. 198-202	

Subject/Reference Matrix

A. Topic	B. Background	C. Scripts	D. Handouts	E. Overheads	F. Learning Activities	G. Tools and Assessments	H. Reinforcement Session
7. Controlling		One-Day Workshop, Modules 3 and 4, pp. 65-79	Controlling, p. 133 The Control Process, p. 134		Delivering Unpopular News, pp. 142-145 Quality Is Below Standard, pp. 149-153 Ignoring the Chain of Command, pp. 155-159	Controlling Survey, pp. 203-207	
8. New Workforce	pp. 18-25	One-Day Workshop, Modules 2 and 3, pp. 63-74			Ignoring the Chain of Command, pp. 155-159		
9. Changing from Industrial Age to Information Age Structures	pp. 25-28	One-Day Workshop Modules 2 and 3, pp. 63-74		Supervisory Job Knowledge, p. 218 Management Skills, p 219	Get-Acquainted Treasure Hunt, pp. 136-137 Ignoring the Chain of Command, pp. 155-159		

Time Block/Methods Matrix

Directions

To select a training method that fits a particular time block, go to Column A and locate the row that lists the time block you wish to fill. Then go across the row to the cell where the desired time block and training method intersect to find the material that meets your criteria. For example, if you want a 45-minute assessment, go to Column A, Row 2 (45-minute time block). Then go to cell 2-C (45-minute assessments) for tools and assessments that meet your time criteria. Also, refer to the Appendix, *Recommended Resources*, for titles of videos/films that fit each time block.

A. Time Block Available	B. Learning Activities	C. Tools and Assessments
1. 30 minutes or less	Get-Acquainted Treasure Hunt, p. 136 He's Sinking Fast, p. 138 Delivering Unpopular News, p. 142 Preserving the Friendship, p. 146 Quality Is Below Standard, p. 149 Ignoring the Chain of Command, p. 155	Self-Appraisal, p. 176 Workforce Trial Balance Worksheet, p. 193 Skill-Application Planning, p. 208 Program Evaluation, p. 212
2. 45 minutes	Delegation Planning, p. 167 Giving Instructions: Extra Mile Athletic Shoes, p. 170	Planning Survey, p. 186 Organizing Survey, p. 194 Leading Survey, p. 198 Controlling Survey, p. 203
3. 1 hour	By adding a skill practice or demonstration, the following discussion cases become one-hour activities: Preserving the Friendship, p. 146 Quality Is Below Standard, p. 149 Ignoring the Chain of Command, p. 155 Going Through the Work Orders, p. 160	Supervisory Roles Assessment, p. 180 The following tools and assessments will fit a one-hour time block when the facilitator commentary and group discussion are expanded: Self-Appraisal, p. 176 Workforce Trial Balance Planning Worksheet, p. 193

Navigating the Training Plans

The training plans are the heart of the seminar and workshop sessions—the glue that draws and holds everything else together. These training plans are set out in detail on a module-by-module basis, with an agenda, statement of purpose, and objectives for each module. We have attempted to make these training plans as easy to use and as complete as possible. A sample with annotations is shown on page 11. The icons are translated on page 10. Look for the following elements in each training plan:

1. Each section within a module has a heading that includes a statement of purpose for the section and suggested timing.

2. Within each section, you will find one or more major activities, each marked by an icon and a descriptive heading.

3. Additionally, you will find a number of supporting activities, each marked with an icon and explained with a suggested action.

4. Suggested actions are shown in conjunction with supporting activities, with the appropriate action verb in *UPPERCASE BOLD ITALIC*.

5. Suggested comments accompany many of the suggested actions. While these comments are fully "scripted," it is not intended that you "parrot" these remarks—but rather paraphrase the key thoughts in a way that is meaningful to you and the participants.

Understanding the Icons

Major Activities

The following icons mark major activities:

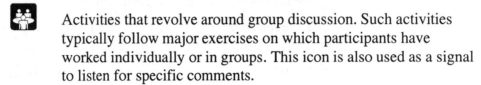 Activities that feature facilitator commentary. In these activities, you—as facilitator—present information that will be key to subsequent workshop activities.

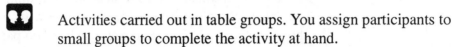 Activities carried out in table groups. You assign participants to small groups to complete the activity at hand.

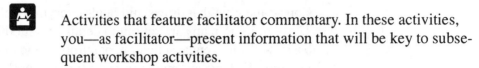 Activities that revolve around group discussion. Such activities typically follow major exercises on which participants have worked individually or in groups. This icon is also used as a signal to listen for specific comments.

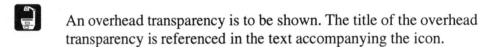 Activities completed on an individual basis.

Supporting Activities

The following icons mark supporting activities:

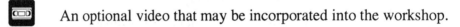 An overhead transparency is to be shown. The title of the overhead transparency is referenced in the text accompanying the icon.

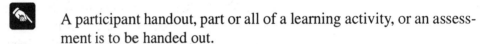 An optional video that may be incorporated into the workshop.

A participant handout, part or all of a learning activity, or an assessment is to be handed out.

A question is to be asked. Wording for the question is provided, as are suggested answers when appropriate.

A flipchart is to be used.

Notes

The following icons mark notes to the facilitator:

Indicates when to call time for timed exercises.

Marks the end of an exercise or section.

Sample Page

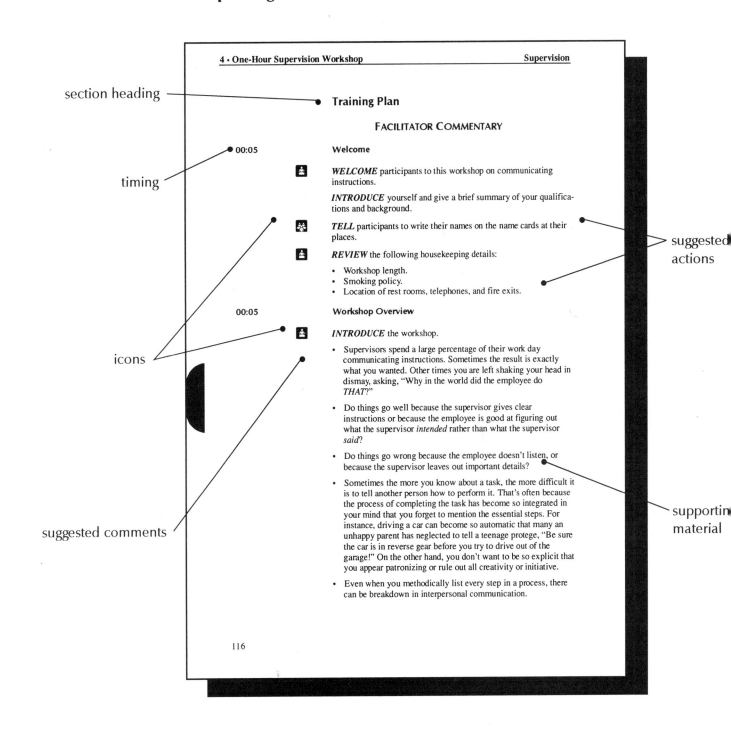

section heading

timing

icons

suggested comments

suggested actions

supporting material

4 · One-Hour Supervision Workshop   **Supervision**

Training Plan

FACILITATOR COMMENTARY

Welcome

00:05

WELCOME participants to this workshop on communicating instructions.

INTRODUCE yourself and give a brief summary of your qualifications and background.

TELL participants to write their names on the name cards at their places.

REVIEW the following housekeeping details:

- Workshop length.
- Smoking policy.
- Location of rest rooms, telephones, and fire exits.

Workshop Overview

00:05

INTRODUCE the workshop.

- Supervisors spend a large percentage of their work day communicating instructions. Sometimes the result is exactly what you wanted. Other times you are left shaking your head in dismay, asking, "Why in the world did the employee do *THAT*?"

- Do things go well because the supervisor gives clear instructions or because the employee is good at figuring out what the supervisor *intended* rather than what the supervisor *said*?

- Do things go wrong because the employee doesn't listen, or because the supervisor leaves out important details?

- Sometimes the more you know about a task, the more difficult it is to tell another person how to perform it. That's often because the process of completing the task has become so integrated in your mind that you forget to mention the essential steps. For instance, driving a car can become so automatic that many an unhappy parent has neglected to tell a teenage protege, "Be sure the car is in reverse gear before you try to drive out of the garage!" On the other hand, you don't want to be so explicit that you appear patronizing or rule out all creativity or initiative.

- Even when you methodically list every step in a process, there can be breakdown in interpersonal communication.

116

Formula for Supervision

This sourcebook gives you the substance—both content and techniques—you need to explain and discuss the basic concepts for your supervision workshops.   While the instructions are not intended to cover every eventuality, experience indicates that with thorough preparation and careful study, you can be ready to lead an effective workshop.

But substance is only one component of a successful workshop. It's up to you to make the material relevant to each audience by combining your energy with appropriate content emphasis and relevant examples. Equally important, you've got to involve participants and kindle their enthusiasm for the topic. When you blend substance with energy, emphasis, examples, and enthusiasm, you have a winning formula for producing high-performance supervisors who add value by helping their enterprises become leaders in our global marketplace.

Chapter Two:

Background

This chapter provides background on changes occurring in the nature of supervision in our new work world. The chapter addresses the importance of high-performance supervision in the fiercely competitive global economy. It describes the effects of organizational downsizings on supervisors, and explains why many supervisors now have greater responsibility than ever before.

The chapter identifies four major segments of the new workforce, as well as two emerging segments, and provides specific techniques that supervisors can use when managing workers from each segment. Finally, the chapter discusses how organizational structures are evolving from Industrial Age hierarchies to Information Age networks. Techniques for supervising in Information Age enterprises are covered. The chapter also contains a glossary of key terms for supervisory training.

HOW TO USE
THE BACKGROUND INFORMATION

This chapter provides the context for your supervision workshops. Use the information to develop your facilitator commentaries and participant handouts when you present workshops for enterprises that are making the transition from Industrial Age structures to Information Age structures.

Supervising in the New Work World

High-Performance Supervision

Supervisors are on the front lines, interacting moment by moment with employees to accomplish the enterprise's work. Each day the supervisor's job becomes more challenging as enterprises strive to maintain the high performance levels essential to survival in a fiercely competitive global economy.

High-performance supervision pulls diverse contributors together into a cohesive team committed to achieving the enterprise's vision. At the same time, high-performance supervision enables each individual to perform at his or her personal best.

High-Performance Management Versus Low-Octane Management

The two lists on the facing page contrast the healthy results of high-performance management on the part of supervisors, middle managers, and executives, with the costly consequences of low-octane management. Most organizations fall somewhere in the middle of the continuum. The high performers are leading-edge, world-class enterprises. Those with low octane ratings are headed downhill unless they change course quickly and radically.

High-Performance Management	Low-Octane Management
• Strong commitment to shared vision.	• Confusion about the enterprise's direction. Individual goals more important than enterprise's goals.
• Information is shared widely. People communicate openly and honestly.	• Information is guarded closely. Rumors abound.
• Trust levels are high.	• People distrust each other's motives. Political maneuvering is common.
• Excellent safety record.	• High accident rates. Insurance claims and lawsuits result.
• Employees develop professionally.	• Employee skills are becoming obsolete. Recruitment and training costs are high due to turnover.
• High employee morale.	• Low morale. High employee stress levels, absenteeism, and sickness.
• People of diverse backgrounds are accepted; their ideas are valued.	• Hiring and promotions often are based on favoritism. Grievances, discrimination complaints, and lawsuits result.
• Cooperative labor relations.	• Strained labor relations, grievances, slowdowns, strikes.
• Able to recruit and retain talented employees and board members.	• Talented employees and board members leave. Difficulty recruiting replacements.
• Facilities and equipment are state-of-the-art and well maintained.	• Facilities and equipment are aging. Downtime and repairs are frequent.
• High productivity.	• Low or marginal productivity.
• Quality products and services delivered on time, within budget, and at competitive prices.	• Poor quality products and service, unmet schedules, cost overruns, and rework cause loss of good business name.
• Innovation blossoms. Work methods and processes improve. New products and services are introduced. New markets are captured.	• Creativity slumps. Innovation lags. Competitive threats ignored. Enterprise loses markets to more agile competitors.
• Strong current profits and excellent projections.	• Poor financial picture.
• The enterprise is a good citizen of the community. Employees act legally, ethically, and in a socially and environmentally conscious manner.	• Short-term interests of the enterprise dictate environmental, social, and ethical decisions. Investigations and legal actions lead to bad publicity.
• Respected by the public, stockholders, and competitors. Employee pride is high.	• Diminished reputation and good will. Employee pride is low.
• Stock appreciating. Investment capital easy to attract.	• Undercapitalized, stock losing ground. Unable to attract capital.
• Strong global competitor.	• Uncompetitive in the global marketplace.
• A bright future.	• A dim future.

Effects of Downsizing on Supervisors

Since the late 1970s, downsizing has decimated the mid-management ranks, doing away with up to half of the management tiers in many organizations. By some estimates, more than two million middle management positions were permanently eliminated during the 1980s. This pruning at the mid-management level has had the following effects on first-line supervisors:

1. **First-line supervisors have more responsibility.**

   Remaining mid-level managers often have two to three times as many direct reports. For instance, a manager who formerly had eight first-line supervisor reports could have twenty or more in a downsized organization. Also, the manager has more paperwork and less clerical support. Consequently, he or she has less time to spend directing the work of first-line supervisors. As a result, first-line supervisors are acting more independently, taking more responsibility, and working harder than ever before.

2. **First-line supervisors are developing policies and strategies.**

   Instead of carrying out orders formulated at the executive level and relayed by middle management, first-line supervisors and their work teams are becoming more involved in developing policies and strategies. They are creating process, product, and service innovations. Additionally, first-line supervisors are working collaboratively across organizational lines for the overall good of the enterprise. In a cascade effect, some rank-and-file workers are handling jobs previously done by the first-line supervisor, such as scheduling work hours and vacations and taking responsibility for process control and quality control for their areas.

3. **Organizing, influencing, and problem-solving skills are increasingly important.**

   Faced with heavier work loads and more complex responsibilities, supervisors are redefining what tasks are critical, and delegating more work to capable employees. They are resisting the temptation to take over when an employee has a problem. Instead, supervisors are building employee skills through coaching. As organizations become less hierarchical and more fluid, supervisors are sharpening their influence skills so they can work collaboratively with peers, upper management, cross-functional teams, suppliers, and customers.

4. There are fewer chances of promotion because there are fewer management levels.

Despite the fact that supervisors are making a greater contribution than ever before, prospects of moving up through the management ranks are greatly diminished. Many supervisors actually welcome this turn of events, because, rather than bowing to external pressures to move up the ladder, they can remain close to their professional discipline, craft, or trade.

Value-Added Supervision

Supervisors are expected to add value to the enterprise in tangible ways. Simply passing information up and down the chain or directing employees to perform tasks is not enough. Supervisors can add value by:

- Identifying value-added steps and non-value-added steps in processes or service chains, and improving the process. A test question is: Would customers be willing to pay for the steps if they knew you were performing them?

- Scrutinizing indirect costs.

- Initiating new projects that have value.

- Connecting the right people with the right information.

- Learning continuously and applying the knowledge.

- Encouraging employees to learn continuously and to apply their knowledge.

- Adding value to information by interpreting it or building on it.

- Adding to the enterprise's knowledge base; for example, streamlining a process after analyzing customer feedback and then sharing the innovation with other work units.

- Redesigning work to take advantage of changing technology.

- Building the enterprise's "memory" by adding knowledge to shared electronic databases.

The New Workforce

Today's workforce comes with a complex mix of hopes, attitudes, and beliefs that supervisors must understand if they are to lead their employees. High-performance supervisors recognize and appreciate the differences and similarities in their employees. Beyond that, high-performance supervisors carefully tailor their communications strategies to fit each individual employee's values, needs, and styles.

In this section of the Sourcebook, we will examine the characteristics of four major workforce segments and two emerging segments. We will also offer strategies that supervisors can use when working with each segment. The four major segments are:

Baby boomers

Camped on a career plateau

The baby boomers represent over one-third of the U.S. population. By virtue of their sheer numbers, they impact on every aspect of life as no previous generation has done. Many boomers are dissatisfied because they are plateaued—stopped in their career tracks.

Layoff survivors

Anxious and angry

Layoff survivors are anxious about job security. They are angry at employers for breaking the implicit contract to provide loyal, competent workers with reliable employment, steady promotions, and good benefits.

Contingent workers

The just-when-needed labor force

Employers are extending the concept of just-in-time manufacturing to create a just-when-needed labor force. Comprising almost 25 percent of the U.S. workforce, contingent workers are part-timers, temporaries, subcontractors, and leased workers who stop at the reception desk daily to obtain a new admittance badge. Supervisors, for their part, wonder how to manage people that don't even officially work for the company.

The diversity mosaic

"I gotta be me."

Today's workforce is a mosaic—a mix of diverse individuals, each clinging tenaciously to his or her proud heritage. Differences are based on race, color, national origin, culture, language, religion, gender, sexual preference, age, physical or mental disabilities, and thinking or personality styles. Beyond that, as enterprises become increasingly transnational, their workforces become more multicultural. The diversity mosaic has a global look, and its theme is, "I gotta be me."

Mobile and global

Within these four major workforce segments are two emerging segments:

- **Geographically dispersed employees.**

- **Job sharers.**

These Information Age employees want flexibility in where and when they work. Fortunately for them, networking technology and mobile office equipment have made decentralized operations more feasible than ever before. Management misgivings about such alternative staffing arrangements still limit their use; but, as reluctance softens, telecommuting and job sharing will come into wider use.

Segments overlap

These segments overlap. It's possible to be a plateaued female baby boomer who has survived a layoff, or an African-American contingent worker who has lost a "permanent" job during a downsizing.

Baby Boomers— Camped on a Career Plateau

Plateauing occurs when an individual reaches a stage in work or life where there is no more growth or movement, according to Judith M. Bardwick, author of *The Plateauing Trap*. It's a time when people feel blocked, especially in their careers, and can't see any way to reach the next step (Judith Bardwick, *The Plateauing Trap: How To Avoid It in Your Career and Your Life*, New York: AMACOM, 1986, pp. 7,11).

Plateauing is a normal part of human development, and most people experience it several times during life. But the problem is reaching epic proportions as some eighty million baby boomers confront discrepancies between their high career expectations and vastly diminished opportunities. Born between 1946 and 1964, the boomers constitute one-third of the U.S. population. They are a well-educated, competitive lot, and they've been granted instant gratification since they were tiny tots. Until now.

The boomers' career expectations and financial goals were shaped by watching their parents climb the corporate ladder. Suddenly they find they may never be as affluent as dad and mom. It's a rude awakening for a group that subscribed wholeheartedly to the American dream of earning a sizable income, owning a spacious home, sending their kids to top schools, and enjoying a comfortable retirement.

Here's what happened

Between 1950 and 1975, the nation experienced a period of sustained economic expansion. With more than enough jobs to go around, good performers moved up quickly, receiving promotions every eighteen to twenty-four months along with regular salary increases.

Beginning in the late 1970s, economic and demographic forces combined to bring about a dramatic shift. In what seemed like an epidemic of mergers and acquisitions, companies reorganized, eliminating duplicate jobs. Automation and robotics led to the phase out of still more jobs, while electronic mail began to circumvent the chain of command. Desperate to compete in the global marketplace, organizations pared down the bureaucracy to slash costs and increase efficiency. "Lean and mean" became the watchword. At the same time, the baby boomers entered the labor market seeking the fast track, only to find the station boarded up.

Motivating boomers

To keep boomers and others motivated in the face of dwindling promotional opportunities, enterprises are making systemic changes. Examples are:

- Using lateral transfers as developmental assignments.

- Offering overseas assignments or special assignments in other domestic locations.

- Restructuring pay grades to allow greater flexibility in giving raises—for instance, creating broader pay bands so workers can qualify for raises when they move sideways instead of taking a salary cut.

- Tying pay to performance, not just seniority or cost of living indices.

- Encouraging employees to make learning a way of life by granting pay increases for attaining and using new skills at work.

- Establishing employer-sponsored child care and elder care centers at or near the work site.

- Redefining work to allow job sharing, telecommuting, flextime, and part-time arrangements.

Supervisors can do their part to keep boomers and other employees from becoming plateaued by:

- Training employees in marketable skills.

- Asking experienced employees to train others.

- Placing employees on interdisciplinary teams or creating special teams within the work unit.

- Reconfiguring duties to add variety and challenge.

- Having candid discussions with employees about their career prospects, including plateauing.
- Emphasizing the positive aspects of slower promotions—for example, more depth and breadth of experience, staying with a project until completion.

Layoff Survivors— Anxious and Angry

After a decade of downsizings, mergers, reorganizations, and relocations, it's clear that in most organizations job security and career advancement are tenuous at best. So, many in the workforce are anxious and angry.

The challenge facing supervisors of layoff survivors is to rebuild their trust in the organization, revitalize their loyalty, and rekindle their motivation. Some strategies follow.

 Meet with survivors individually.

Brief them on plans for the work team. Let them know that they are valuable team members, and explain how they fit in. Listen and respond to their concerns and feelings. Ask for their support.

 Meet with the entire work team.

Discuss issues that affect the group, such as where the organization is headed, how the work unit fits in, and how the group will function as a team.

 Seek the team's ideas about operating methods.

If survivors have to shoulder additional responsibilities, seek their ideas. Ask employees to identify functions and place them in one of three categories:

- Must do.
- Could do.
- Discontinue.

Also, give employees the opportunity to state which assignments they prefer.

 Treat employees as stakeholders.

Keep them informed about how well the enterprise is doing. Being candid builds trust.

As supervisors work with their teams to redistribute duties and restore trust, they should coordinate closely with upper management. Supervisors must stay within the limits of their authority, and the plans they develop must meet upper management's approval.

Contingent Workers—
The Just-When-Needed Labor Force

Many employers are moving away from maintaining large full-time labor forces. Instead, they employ more part-timers. Beyond that, they contract out, or outsource, jobs to agencies that provide temporary, subcontracted, or leased workers.

In contrast to the full-time or "core" labor force, these temporary workers are called the contingent or flexible workforce. By some estimates, they comprised about 25 percent of the workforce in 1993, and could swell to nearly half the workforce by the year 2000 (Beverly Geber, "The Flexible Workforce: Using Contingent Workers Wisely and Humanely," *Training*, December 1993, p. 24).

The trend is a mixed blessing for the first-line supervisor. On the positive side, it allows the supervisor to staff up for peak production periods or to cover for a regular employee who is on vacation, sick leave, or family leave. Many contingent workers are stellar. They bring top notch skills and apply themselves diligently in hopes of good recommendations, or, even better, a core position at the company. Also, temporary workers can be a source of fresh ideas and enthusiasm.

Yet, most contingent workers need orientation and training. And, it may take a while before they are fully productive. Some temps, lacking a long-term stake in the organization, may have only tepid motivation and commitment.

When low wage temporaries perform the same work as higher paid core employees, conflict can result. Also, when core employees compensated on the basis of output urge contingent employees paid by the hour to work faster, tempers can flare.

Instead of contracting with temporary employment agencies, many organizations establish in-house pools of employees who float from one department to another, depending on staffing needs. This arrangement eases concerns about workers' loyalty and motivation. It also removes questions about the extent to which the organization should supervise and train employees. But, first-line supervisors are still faced with the challenge of managing temporary workers and assimilating them into the work group for short periods.

In the December 1993 issue of *Training* magazine, Beverly Geber offers suggestions for utilizing talents of contingent workers (Geber, pp. 29-30).

Supervising contingent workers

Some of her ideas are listed below:

- If you plan to bring a temporary employee on board, meet with core employees first. Explain why the temp is needed, and assure them that their jobs are not in jeopardy.

- Treat the temporary employee like a team member. You'll get better performance from someone who feels an attachment to the organization.

- Don't give temporary employees the most undesirable work. If they feel exploited, they may not put forth their best efforts.

- Plan ahead. Sufficient lead times will allow you to find well trained, high caliber temps.

The Diversity Mosaic— "I gotta be me."

Our workforce is becoming more diverse. Differences can be based on race, color, national origin, culture, language, religion, gender, sexual preference, age, physical or mental disabilities, and thinking or personality styles. The result is that everyone in the workplace must show greater respect for and tolerance of differences.

Bridging differences

Supervisors can take the following steps to bridge differences:

- To prevent misunderstandings, use simple language, explain with show-and-tell techniques, and ask employees to demonstrate their understanding via show-and-tell.

- To mediate when conflicts arise between employees, learn about other cultures and use problem-solving and conflict-management skills.

- Identify informal leaders among the immigrant workers and enlist their help in resolving problems.

- Lead by example. Treat all people with dignity and respect.

Generational diversity is responsible for a cross section of values about work, manners, dress, ethics, and life styles. Ken Dychtwald, author of *Age Wave*, predicts that inter-generational relationship skills will be critical in the years ahead. For instance, supervisors in their twenties will have to learn how to effectively manage workers twice their age. Similarly, workers in their fifties will have to accept direction from managers many years their junior ("The Age Wave: An Interview With Ken Dychtwald," *Training and Development Journal*, February 1990, p. 30).

To influence and motivate workers from three or four different generations, supervisors can do the following:

- Individualize rewards based on employee values and career goals.

- Draw on the experience and knowledge base that older employees have. These employees are keen observers, but often they don't volunteer information or suggestions out of respect for their younger manager. Supervisors who seek insights from older workers can gain valuable information from this rich reservoir.

- Ask senior employees to serve as coaches for more junior people.

- To keep employees of all ages vitalized, provide training, reinforcement, and retraining.

No matter what the source of diversity, the supervisor's ability to understand and motivate people with different backgrounds, values, and special needs is crucial to productivity.

For diversity training designs and materials, see *DIVERSITY: The ASTD Trainer's Sourcebook* by Tina Rasmussen, a companion volume in the Trainer's Sourcebook series.

Mobile and Global

Supervisors can expect an increase in requests for alternative staffing arrangements such as telecommuting and job sharing.

Geographically dispersed

Geographically dispersed employees work off-site. They may be salespeople operating from their cars, field representatives at remote domestic or foreign locations, or individuals who telecommute from home. It is estimated that by the year 2000, over 20 percent of the workforce will telecommute (Ken Dychtwald with Joe Flower, *Age Wave: The Challenges and Opportunities of an Aging America*, New York: Bantam Books, 1990, p. 198).

Job sharing

Job sharing allows two or more people to occupy a single position. In the case of two individuals, one might work solo on Monday and Tuesday, the other on Thursday and Friday. For coordination, they would both be on-site on Wednesdays.

Even though telecommuters and other geographically dispersed employees work off-site and job sharers typically work on-site, these staffing arrangements raise similar issues. These include how to communicate, make assignments, coordinate work, give direction, meet deadlines, and provide quality customer service when an employee rarely is at the same work site as the supervisor and co-workers.

Telecommuting and job sharing work best for both employer and employee when supervisors take the following steps:

- Collaborate with the employee(s) to develop a work plan with specific goals and quantifiable measurements of accomplishments. Agree on dates for deliverables.

- Inform other staff members about the arrangements.

- Communicate, communicate, communicate. Keep geographically dispersed employees posted on happenings at the main office, and make them responsible for staying in contact, as well.

- Schedule regular team meetings that include geographically dispersed employees or job sharers.

- Rotate geographically dispersed workers back to headquarters now and then.

- Continually evaluate the success of telecommuting and job sharing arrangements.

Shifting from Industrial Age to Information Age Structures

We are living and working in a period of transition from the Industrial Age, where the source of wealth was labor, capital, and natural resources, to the Information Age, where the source of wealth is knowledge and human capital (capable people). Consequently, many enterprises are redesigning their structures in order to be more competitive in the new economy. However, the pace of transition differs markedly from one enterprise to another.

Evolving from Pyramids to Networks

One of the major differences between Industrial Age and Information Age enterprises is that the former are hierarchical and the latter are networked. As organizations evolve from Industrial Age hierarchies to Information Age networks, their structures are becoming more flexible and their approaches to management more collaborative.

In a hierarchy or bureaucratic enterprise, the formal organization chart looks like a pyramid. Precise boxes show levels; straight lines connect each box with those directly above, below, and across. The lines define reporting levels—the chain of command; and they illustrate how communication officially flows down, up, and across the enterprise.

As we move from the Industrial Age to the Information Age, the hierarchy is giving way to web-like human networks linked electronically. Extensions of the old-boy and old-girl networks, today's high tech networks crisscross organizational boundaries, providing direct access to people and information.

Industrial Age organizations are under substantial pressures to change from hierarchical structures to networked ones. Each of the developments cited below represents an erosion of the pyramid and an emergence of the network.

1. **Wide use of information technology.**

   Networking technology, electronic mail, shared databases, and group decision-making software make decentralized operations and direct communication feasible.

2. **Enterprises have fewer tiers in their structures.**

   To compete in a world economy, businesses have cut costs relentlessly, and mid-management jobs were easy targets. Whole tiers in bureaucracies were done away with, leading to the exodus of over two million managers during the 1980s. As pyramids began to look more like pancakes, employees gained latitude to communicate across organizational boundaries and to make decisions on their own.

3. **Speed is a competitive advantage.**

   Speed in product development, distribution, and customer service is crucial to obtaining and retaining market share. The hierarchy, with its sluggish response time, is being supplanted by cross-functional concurrent engineering teams for product development and electronic data interchange for communication with customers and suppliers.

4. **Employee empowerment is essential for quality and customer satisfaction.**

   To achieve the world-class quality standards and continuous improvement demanded by the global marketplace, companies are empowering workers on the line to identify and solve problems, as well as to constantly improve processes. Similarly, to keep customers happy, enterprises are giving customer service representatives authority to solve problems on the spot. In many situations, the buck stops with the front-line employee, rather than being passed up the chain of command.

5. **Employees want to participate as team members.**

Young, well-educated, computer-literate employees chafe under strict chains of command and authoritarian supervision. They expect to participate as team members, not be treated as subordinates. They want to communicate across organizational boundaries, not be fenced in by them. E-mail lets them do just that.

6. **Knowledge work happens in the mind, not the office.**

Knowledge work is difficult to supervise. Results are visible, but supervisors can't watch the creative process that occurs in the employee's mind, often at unpredictable times or in places other than an office cubicle. In a networked organization, an employee sitting in his cozy home study wearing a robe and slippers might log on at midnight for a couple of hours' productive work. Offices are becoming flexplaces linked by telecommunications.

Changing nature of supervision

Supervisors in bureaucracies are links between operating employees and mid-level management, sending information down and back up the chain of command. In networked organizations, supervisors facilitate and coordinate work processes from the center of a web of relationships. Those webs stretch far beyond organizational or even national boundaries to encompass direct reports, peers, upper management, subject matter experts, suppliers, customers, and professional colleagues anywhere on the globe.

Workers have more autonomy and receive less direct supervision in networked environments than in bureaucracies. Supervisors, acting as coaches, are more concerned with an employee's overall performance than with giving detailed instructions about small parcels of work.

Teams—A Middle Ground

Teams, a frequent mechanism for stimulating employee involvement, stand on middle ground between a rigid hierarchy and a networked organization. *Training* magazine's 1993 industry survey indicates that 76 percent of U.S. organizations now call some of their working groups "teams." Among organizations with teams, 38 percent classify some of their teams as self-managed, self-directing, or semi-autonomous. Typically, self-managing teams consist of five to fifteen multiskilled employees who rotate jobs and produce an entire product or service.

On such teams, members assume many of the functions previously considered the province of management, including setting work schedules and production quotas, monitoring quality and quantity of work, dealing directly with external customers, giving performance feedback to teammates, and selecting new talent for the team. ("The Teaming of America," *Training*, October 1993, pp. 58-59.) Also, teams are expected to suggest innovative ideas for improved processes, products, and services.

To stimulate innovation and shorten product development times, enterprises establish cross-functional concurrent engineering teams. Such teams are composed of representatives from the major functions involved in the innovation process. For instance, research and development, engineering, manufacturing, sales, marketing, customers, and suppliers work collaboratively to bring an idea to the marketplace. Then most team members go on to other assignments. With concurrent engineering teams, product development cycles are shortened dramatically, because specialists in each function work on an innovation simultaneously rather than sequentially.

Cooperation is essential to team success. Leadership usually is shared, with members reporting to and depending on each other. Often the role of formal leader is rotated among members. Teammates expect each other to fulfill commitments, as well as to be reliable agents for both the team and their home departments.

For training designs on teamwork, see *TEAMBUILDING: The ASTD Trainer's Sourcebook* by Cresencio Torres and Deborah M. Fairbanks.

Effective team supervision

Supervisors, for their part, facilitate the work of empowered employees and project teams by:

 Coaching less experienced members.
Coach less experienced employees so that they gain the competence to act independently.

 Keeping focused on strategic vision.
Help teams keep projects aligned with the organization's strategic vision.

 Keeping teams well-informed.
Bring teams together periodically for progress updates and discussions of critical issues.

 Offering practical guidance.
Guide teams in problem-solving, decision-making, and conflict resolution processes.

 Nurturing creativity.
Nurture creativity and inspire innovation.

 Selling team ideas.
Help to sell the team's innovative ideas.

 Negotiating.
Negotiate for resources.

 Networking and attracting new business.
Develop networks to keep communication channels open and attract new business.

 Encouraging continuous learning.
Help individuals and teams engage in continuous learning by obtaining new skills, unlearning old ways, and relearning as change dictates.

 Providing opportunities for team visibility.
Give teams opportunities to gain visibility and to share their learning; for example, by giving briefings.

Preserving the team's knowledge base.
Ensure that the knowledge-base developed within the unit is documented and added to electronic databases, so others can benefit from and build upon the learning.

Key Terms

Accountability	Being held answerable for results.
Authority	Power that gives a supervisor the right to make decisions, carry out actions, and direct others. Organizational authority flows down the chain of command.
Chain of command	Formal channel that specifies the hierarchical authority, responsibility, and communications relationships in an organization. Individuals higher on the chain have more authority than those below them.
Charisma	Leadership quality that captures popular imagination and inspires devotion.
Contingent workers	Part-time, temporary, subcontracted and leased employees.
Controlling	(1) Process of setting standards, measuring performance against those standards, and correcting unwanted deviations. (2) Fourth step in the supervision process of planning, organizing, leading, and controlling.
Core competency	What an enterprise does best.
Core employees	Key employees that the enterprise wants to employ because they possess critical skills.
Delegation	Assignment of responsibilities and obligations to others, along with authority and resources necessary to complete the job.
Goals	End results.
Key Result Areas (KRAs)	Subject areas where high performance is essential to fulfillment of the unit's mission.
Knowledge	Awareness or comprehension acquired by experience or study.

Leading   (1) Process of influencing others to follow in the achievement of a common goal. (2) Third step in the supervision process of planning, organizing, leading, and controlling.

Line managers   Oversee line functions, which are activities central to producing the enterprise's products and services, for instance, engineering, production, and manufacturing.

Network   (1) Electronic system that interconnects people and computers. An essential component of the Information Age infrastructure. (2) Personal relationship system that links people with common concerns to one another for information exchange and mutual support.

Objectives   Actions or tasks that must be accomplished to achieve a goal.

Organizing   (1) Manner in which supervisors organize tasks and people to accomplish work. (2) Way in which management designs the structure of an enterprise. (3) Second step in the supervision process of planning, organizing, leading, and controlling.

Outsourcing   Contracting with outside firms for services that were previously performed by in-house employees.

Parity principle   Authority and responsibility must coincide.

Personal power   Power based on personal characteristics that cause others to follow a particular individual or leader.

Planning   (1) Process of envisioning the future, setting goals, identifying actions to achieve the goals, establishing completion dates, and describing measures of success. (2) First step in the supervision process of planning, organizing, leading, and controlling.

Plateauing	A normal part of human development that occurs when an individual reaches a stage in work or life where there is no more growth or movement.
Position power	Power derived from the formal authority that accompanies a position such as a managerial post.
Power	Ability to influence the behavior of others, for example, to gain commitment or compliance from others.
Responsibilities	Duties for which one is held accountable.
Self-directing teams	Teams that perform functions previously considered the province of management, for example, setting work schedules and production quotas, monitoring quality, and giving performance feedback to teammates.
Skill	Proficiency at performing a task.
Specification	A collection of standardized dimensions and characteristics pertaining to a product, process, or service.
Staff managers	Direct units that support the line organization by performing analyses, advising, or providing internal services; for instance, human resources, legal, public relations, administrative services, or materials management.
Standard	Measure or basis for judging performance.
Tolerance	Leeway from the standard.
Variance	The gap between actual performance and the standard of performance.

Chapter Three:

Workshop Preparation

Workshops which flow so smoothly they appear effortless to the casual observer are almost always the result of thorough preparation and careful attention to details.

GETTING READY

This chapter contains general tips on how to prepare for your supervision workshop, including:

- Managing your own training program.
- Getting Ready.
- Presentation Checklist.
- Facilitator Preparation.
- Conducting the Workshop.
- Workshop Follow-Up.

The chapter also contains a *Workshop Agenda Template* for blocking out the flow of your workshop. In addition, to help you remember the myriad of details associated with planning and delivering a workshop, we have included a comprehensive checklist.

Designing Your Own Training Program

To design your own training program, you must define the client's needs, determine program content, and select methods and media.

Defining Client Needs

The first step in designing a training program is to determine the client's needs. The four factors listed below define the parameters within which you must design your workshop.

1. **Participants' training needs.**

   Workshop content must meet participants' training needs. Ideally, needs are determined through an assessment process where actual employee knowledge and skills are compared with industry standards or other criteria. If deficiencies or needs are discovered, and if training can remedy the situation, then the enterprise arranges for the necessary training.

2. **Time available for training.**

   Supervision is a broad topic. You can dip into one aspect in sixty minutes, give a one-day overview, or build a wide range of skills through a forty-hour program. Program length generally depends upon how long supervisors can be away from the job, as well as training costs.

3. **Training budget.**

   The training budget will have a significant impact on the program length, number of trainees, training site, materials, equipment, and type of media used.

4. **Class size and composition.**

   Class size and composition will influence your choice of instructional methods, media, and content. If you plan small group discussions and skill practice, limit the class to between fifteen and thirty people. The larger or more participative the group, the longer it will take to cover each topic. The smaller or more reserved the group, the more quickly the workshop will move.

Determining Program Content

Once you know the participants' training needs, the length of the program, your budget, and the size and composition of the class, you are ready to select the workshop content. In conjunction with your client, you must decide:

- What content meets the client's training objectives within the time and budget available.

- What content level is suitable for the class size and composition.

- How to sequence the information. Studying Chapters 1, 2 and 7 will help you to select and sequence program content. Break the workshop subjects into teachable components or units that proceed from the simple to the complex, the known to the unknown. Use the participants' existing knowledge base as your point of departure and build on that platform as you introduce new material. Also, relate the content to what participants do on the job.

Selecting Training Methods and Media

Once you've determined the workshop content and presentation sequence, you will be ready to select training methods and media. Methods are the techniques you use to teach the concepts and skills. Media are materials that illustrate the ideas being presented. Training methods and media must support the training objectives, fit the time block available, and be appropriate to the size and composition of the group. Training methods and media are described below.

Methods

The methods listed below are employed in the one-day, half-day, and one-hour training agendas contained in this sourcebook.

Facilitator commentary

Your facilitator commentaries are the threads that hold the workshop together. Use commentaries of up to ten minutes to present key concepts or background information. When you give a commentary, follow the instructor adage: Tell them what you're going to tell them; tell them; and tell them what you told them.

Keep your commentaries lively by interspersing questions and answers. Alternate commentaries with exercises that require participants to apply knowledge or practice a skill. To make your material captivating and memorable, use humor, personal anecdotes, and relevant examples.

Give commentaries of between one and five minutes to bridge between one training method and another. For instance, if you have just completed small group discussions and are about to begin a skill practice, your commentary could summarize the learning gained during the small group discussions and introduce the skill practice.

Question and answer

The question and answer technique draws out the group's knowledge, keeps participants alert, creates involvement, and allows the facilitator to verify participants' understanding of concepts.

Individual activities

Individual activities include readings, written exercises, self-assessments, action planning, and knowledge-based tests. Individual activities allow participants to work at their own pace and on their own agendas. Some people will complete their work more quickly than others. When this occurs, have a supplemental assignment for the early finishers.

Small group discussions and reports

Small group discussions involve participants and allow them to apply what they have learned. Discussions also give shy members a safe forum for contributing ideas. To use this method, assign participants to groups of two to six people, and give them a discussion topic. Ask them to create charts for posting, and tell them to be prepared to give a brief report to the entire class. Throughout the day, form groups of various sizes so that participants will have the opportunity to work with different people.

Skill practice and feedback

Participants practice the concepts, skills, and techniques presented in the workshop and receive feedback from other participants and from the facilitator. Shy or reserved individuals sometimes resist skill practice. If you have a group that you think will be reticent about participating in a skill practice, use discussion cases or a front-of-the-room demonstration instead.

Demonstrations

Give two participants a scenario involving an employee and a supervisor, and ask them to demonstrate the interaction. The success of a demonstration depends heavily on the skill levels of the individuals giving the demonstration; so, select the participants carefully.

Self-assessments

Self-assessments are individual activities that allow participants to evaluate their use of certain behaviors. The results reveal strengths and areas for development, as well as provide the participant with a baseline against which to measure change.

Action planning

Participants plan to apply their new skills when they return to the workplace by setting developmental goals and implementation dates.

Media

The media listed below are recommended for use in conjunction with the workshops described in this sourcebook.

Overhead transparencies

Overhead transparencies help the audience follow your presentation, and they help you stay on track, as well. Keep transparencies simple—no more than five lines on a horizontal format or seven lines on a vertical format. Use a clean, solid 24-point typeface that can be read from the back of the room.

Charts

Facilitators with good artistic and lettering skills can enliven their presentations with 2-foot by 3-foot flipcharts displayed on an easel stand or posted on a wall. Facilitators with poor lettering skills serve their students and themselves better by showing typeset overhead transparencies. Charts are excellent for recording information generated during the workshop. Use charts in small rooms where they can be seen by all.

Printed handouts

Handouts give participants permanent reference material, and minimize the need for notetaking. To facilitate distribution and use, put all your handouts (except those where you want an element of surprise) in a packet with numbered pages, and pass it out at the beginning of the workshop. In addition to receiving detailed reference material, participants also appreciate having copies of your overhead transparencies.

Videos/films

Videos and films are used as options in this sourcebook's training plans to present concepts, illustrate how concepts can be applied by dramatizing interactions, and show positive behavior models. Through video, participants can learn from subject matter experts who might not be available in person, either because of their schedule or your training budget.

As a general rule, show only one video per half-day session. Possible exceptions include session openers or closers that are five minutes or less, and stop-and-go videos that are designed to be viewed in short segments followed by discussion and/or skill practice. Never show a film or video immediately after lunch unless it's a real spellbinder or uproariously funny.

Keep the Spotlight Moving

To keep participants' energy and interest levels high, vary your methods and media. In an effective training program, the spotlight moves around the room. During facilitator commentaries, the spotlight shines on the trainer. During a demonstration, one or two participants share the limelight. When someone is serving as a small group spokesperson, she has center stage.

Students learn best when they participate actively. If you try to carry the entire workshop load, you'll end up with a raspy throat, sore feet, and drowsy students. Allow the spotlight to travel around the room and you'll have enthusiastic, active learners. Equally important, you'll maintain the high energy level required to be at your best for the entire workshop.

Getting Ready

There are a number of administrative functions to perform prior to and after the workshop. Experienced facilitators find the best way to keep track of all the details is with checklists similar to the one on pages 39-40. While you may not want every item on the list for every workshop, you can use this list as a starting point to develop a personalized version that suits your needs exactly.

You don't have to perform all these functions yourself. Often there is an administrative support person on the employee training and development staff who can take responsibility for many administrative tasks. Likewise, if the meeting is being held at a hotel or conference center, a member of the sales and catering staff can oversee room, food service, and audiovisual equipment arrangements. Of course, you will still need close coordination and diligent follow-up to ensure a successful program.

Use the *Workshop Agenda Template* on page 41 to block out your programs and to plan what training methods and media best suit your training objectives.

Presentation Checklist

Program title: _____

Program date: _____ Time: _____

Name of facilitator: _____

Location: _____

Number of participants: _____

Administration

☐ Schedule meeting site

☐ Determine furniture arrangement

☐ Determine food and beverage service

☐ Determine access time and method

☐ Distribute workshop announcements

☐ Send participant confirmations

Participant Materials

☐ Name tags or tent cards

☐ Handouts

☐ Copies of facilitator's biographical sketch (1 page)

☐ Pens or pencils

☐ Ruled paper

☐ Evaluations

☐ Hard candy or mints

☐ Prizes

Trainer Materials

☐ Workshop agenda

☐ Training plan

☐ Overhead transparencies

☐ Videos/Films

☐ 2' by 3' chart pads

☐ Hand-lettered charts

☐ Felt-tip markers

☐ Transparency pens

☐ Masking tape

☐ Cellophane tape

☐ Dry-erase markers

☐ Chalk

☐ Erasers

☐ Three-hole punch

☐ Staples

☐ Staple puller

Equipment

☐ Overhead projector

☐ Screen

☐ Easel(s)

☐ Video player and monitor

    ☐ 1/2" VHS

    ☐ 1/2" Beta

    ☐ 3/4" U-matic

☐ Connecting cables

☐ Cart for video equipment

☐ 16 mm. film projector

☐ Cart for projector

☐ Take-up reel of sufficient diameter to hold film

☐ Extension cords

☐ Adaptor plugs

☐ Spare projector lamps

☐ Pointer

☐ Chalkboard

☐ Whiteboard

☐ Podium

☐ Lectern

☐ Microphone(s)

☐ Name of technician: _____ Phone: _____

Other

☐ _____

☐ _____

☐ _____

Workshop Agenda Template

Use this generic workshop agenda template to block out your programs and plan what methods and media to use.

Agenda	Topics, Key Points	Time Allotted	Start	Stop	Training Method	Media	Sourcebook Pages
1. Start-up	• Welcome • Housekeeping						
2. Agenda	• Schedule • Key topics • Objectives						
3. Introductions							
4. Icebreaker							
5. Core material							
6. Break							
7. Core material							
8. Lunch							
9. Energizer							
10. Core material							
11. Break							
12. Core material							
13. Evaluations							
14. Adjourn							

Workshop Announcement

Announce the workshop at least four weeks prior to the scheduled date. You can publicize the program via memos, letters, E-mail, voice mail, personal phone calls, announcements at meetings, employee newspaper, or management bulletin. Include the following information:

- Workshop title.

- Date and hours of the workshop.

- Location.

- Description.

- Objectives.

- Key topics.

- Prerequisites (if any).

- Facilitator's name and brief statement of credentials.

- Cost.

- How to apply.

- Application deadline.

A sample participant roster is provided on page 43. Record enrollment requests on a photocopy of this sheet. When the list is finalized, create an alphabetized roster to serve as a workshop sign-in sheet. To prepare a name tent and a certificate of achievement for each participant, use the reproducible masters on pages 44 and 52, respectively.

Participant Roster

Workshop Title: _____

Trainer(s): _____

Date: _____   **Time:** _____

Location: _____

_____

	Participant Name	**Extension**	**Department**
1.	_____	_____	_____
2.	_____	_____	_____
3.	_____	_____	_____
4.	_____	_____	_____
5.	_____	_____	_____
6.	_____	_____	_____
7.	_____	_____	_____
8.	_____	_____	_____
9.	_____	_____	_____
10.	_____	_____	_____
11.	_____	_____	_____
12.	_____	_____	_____
13.	_____	_____	_____
14.	_____	_____	_____
15.	_____	_____	_____
16.	_____	_____	_____
17.	_____	_____	_____
18.	_____	_____	_____
19.	_____	_____	_____
20.	_____	_____	_____

Name Tent

High-Performance Supervision Workshop

Participant Name

High-Performance Supervision Workshop

Participant Name

Facilities and Furniture

Room setup depends on the group's size and room's physical characteristics. Three possible configurations are:

1. **U-shape**

   The U-shape is recommended for ten to twenty people. Avoid seating people on the inside of the U.

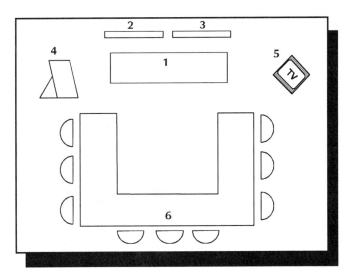

2. **Angled rows**

   Suitable for groups of twenty or more. Arrange rectangular tables seating two or three people in a chevron pattern. Leave aisles that are wide enough for you to move about the room comfortably.

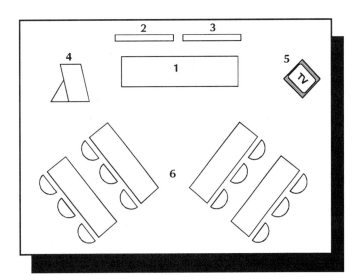

3. Round tables

Round tables that seat four to five people are suitable for groups of twelve or more. Place chairs so that each participant faces the front of the room.

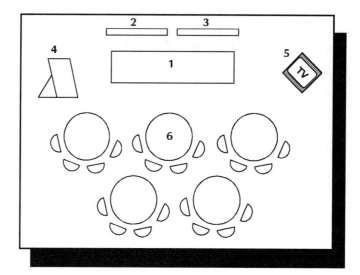

Legend

1. Facilitator's table
2. Whiteboard
3. Projection screen
4. Flipchart stand
5. Video player/monitor
6. Participant tables and seating

Audiovisual equipment

The facilitator's table, easels, and videocassette player should be positioned for clear viewing by all participants. The sound system should be adjusted so that everyone can hear videos, films, or words spoken into a microphone.

Power source

Find out where the climate control, light switches, electrical outlets, and sound system controls are. Also, obtain the name of the technician to call if you need assistance.

Supplies and refreshments

Place one table to the side for materials, supplies, and items such as a three-hole punch, stapler, and staple puller. If refreshments will be served, set those up on a second side table.

Facilities

Locate the phones, rest rooms, vending machines, and cafeteria so that you can direct participants to them. Get names of nearby lunch spots if lunch is not provided.

Facilitator Preparation

Follow these steps to prepare to facilitate the workshop:

1. Review the sourcebook to become familiar with the background material, training designs, handouts, overhead transparency masters, learning activities, and assessments and tools.

2. Review your workshop plans with your client.

3. Select and duplicate handout masters from Chapter 7.

4. Select and duplicate transparency masters from Chapter 10.

5. Create hand-lettered charts.

6. Preview any films or videos, and read the accompanying leader's guides.

7. Practice and time your remarks, using a videotape recorder, audiotape, or mirror as a feedback device. Better yet, rehearse your presentation before a few colleagues who can provide constructive suggestions.

8. Learn to operate the audiovisual equipment, and make sure the equipment reserved for you works.

On the Day of the Workshop

 Arrive 30 to 40 minutes early.
Give yourself enough time to take care of all necessary details—including the unexpected. Make sure to allow a few moments for yourself before the participants arrive.

 Test the audiovisual equipment.
Make sure that you are familiar with the audiovisual equipment, and that it is in working order, positioned properly, and in focus.

 Check to see that the video or film is cued properly.
Videos and film, if used, should be positioned at the starting point, ready to play.

Conducting the Workshop

The following pages describe some general techniques on workshop facilitation.

Build Rapport

To build rapport with the participants:

☑ **Extend a warm welcome.**
Welcome participants with a warm smile and a handshake.

☑ **Call people by name.**
Learn and use participants' first names.

☑ **Show interest.**
Express interest in each individual. Find out what your students want to learn.

☑ **Relax and have fun.**
Show your sense of humor.

☑ **Be approachable.**
Be available to participants at breaks and lunch.

☑ **Look and listen.**
Watch for participants' nonverbal messages such as puzzled looks or signs of discomfort. Listen to their comments and acknowledge their contributions.

Establish Your Credibility

☑ **Look professional.**
Wear clean, pressed clothing that reflects the dress standards of the organization, the group you are training, and the training site. Pay attention to your hair, nails, and makeup, too. Good grooming creates a neat appearance that helps establish professional credibility.

☑ **Know your subject.**
Study the background information in Chapter 2, the workshop scripts, and the directions for facilitating the learning activities and the assessments and tools.

☑ **Speak clearly, distinctly, smoothly, and with authority.**
Avoid slang, jargon, profanity, or other language that might offend. Verbal qualifiers such as "kind of" or "sort of" detract from your credibility. "Ums" and "ahs" convey the impression that you are unsure of your material.

Maintain good posture.
Communicate self-confidence and high self-esteem nonverbally by maintaining good posture.

 Maintain eye contact.
Look participants in the eye when you address them, as well as when you listen to their comments.

 Use gestures for emphasis.
Use gestures to underscore a key point or to make a story come alive.

Showing Overhead Transparencies

Glance at the screen to verify that the overhead transparency is positioned on the projector properly. Place a pen or pointer on the transparency next to the words or images that you want to emphasize. Alternatively, direct the viewers' attention to the screen behind you with the aid of a pointer, while continuing to face your audience. If you talk to the screen, participants won't be able to hear your comments.

Leading Discussions

Discussion questions and suggested answers can be found in the scripts for the one-day, half-day, and one-hour workshop, as well as in the directions that accompany the learning activities and the tools and assessments. Some techniques for leading discussions follow.

 Encourage idea exchange.
Encourage participants to share ideas, experiences, supervision techniques, and systems knowledge, as well as to exchange opinions.

 Involve everyone.
Draw out shy or quiet individuals by giving them assignments; for instance, ask them to serve as recorder of the small group discussions.

 Stay focused on the topic.
Keep discussions focused on the topic. If a comment is off the subject, redirect it. You can also offer to discuss the matter further during a break. If the point is on a topic that you will cover later, defer its discussion.

Keep discussions positive.

Keep discussions positive and constructive. If participants complain about their bosses or about the enterprise's policies, let them ventilate briefly. Then acknowledge their feelings and direct attention back to the workshop objectives, saying something like, "It sounds like you find your situation frustrating. However, we can't change (the organization's policy, your boss's management style, etc.). So, let's put those issues aside and focus on our workshop topics. Look for ways to apply what you are learning today to your work unit."

Questions and Answers

The scripted workshops and many of the learning activities include questions you can ask, along with supporting answers. Some techniques for facilitating question-and-answer sessions follow.

- Ask for volunteers to respond to questions.

- When someone gives an incorrect response, be tactful to avoid causing embarrassment. Often, you can thank the respondent and continue accepting answers from others. When the preferred answers are given, support those answers. If letting an incorrect answer stand will misguide the students, then set the record straight diplomatically.

When participants ask you questions:

- Answer, but don't get carried off the subject.

- Instead of answering, pose the question to the group, encouraging participants to answer for each other.

- If you are unable to provide an answer, say so. Offer alternatives such as asking if others know the answer, suggesting where the participant might find an answer, or promising to obtain the information.

Maintain the Schedule

To cover all the workshop material within the allotted time, it is essential to stay on schedule. During group exercises, circulate and participate briefly in each group's discussions. This keeps the participants alert and ensures that they are completing the assignment. If a group is proceeding slowly relative to the other teams, urge it to pick up the pace.

Workshop Follow-Up

The following post-workshop activities help reinforce the training for each participant—and begin the preparation process for subsequent workshops:

 Tabulate participant evaluations and provide your client with the results.

A sample evaluation for the participants to complete at the conclusion of the workshop can be found on page 212 in Chapter 9, Tools and Assessments.

 Keep material current.

Make any necessary changes before delivering the workshop again.

 Mail participants' action plans.

If you collected copies of participants' action plans, mail them as reminders of their self-binding contracts.

 Plan reinforcement sessions.

To be most effective, a reinforcement session should be planned as an integral part of the workshop.

Workshop Certificate

Certificate of Achievement

This certifies that

_____
(name)

successfully completed the

*High-Performance
Supervision Workshop*

on

_____
(date)

Congratulations!

_____
(Facilitator)

_____
(Training Manager)

Chapter Four

One-Day Supervision Workshop

This chapter contains the training plan for your one-day supervision workshop—ready to go "as is" or to be tailored to meet your needs. The chapter is divided into three parts:

- Workshop Agenda.

- Getting Ready.

- Training Plan.

"HIGH-PERFORMANCE SUPERVISION"

This workshop is designed for new supervisors or for individuals considering supervision as a career option. The workshop also serves as a refresher for more experienced supervisors. The purpose of the workshop is to:

- Communicate the importance of high-performance supervision.

- Identify the basics of supervision.

- Describe challenges facing new supervisors.

- Provide strategies for dealing with these challenges.

- Help new supervisors develop a support network.

Workshop Agenda

1. Workshop Overview	Minutes 45	Start/Stop 8:00 / 8:45	Actual Start / Stop
Welcome	5	8:00 / 8:05	_____ / _____
Workshop Overview	5	8:05 / 8:10	_____ / _____
Paired Participant Introductions	35	8:10 / 8:45	_____ / _____

2. High-Performance Supervision	Minutes 1 hr. 15	Start/Stop 8:45 / 10:00	Actual Start / Stop
High-Performance Supervision versus Low-Octane Supervision	60	8:45 / 9:45	_____ / _____
Break	15	9:45 / 10:00	_____ / _____

3. The Basics of Supervision	Minutes 1 hr. 50	Start/Stop 10:00 / 11:50	Actual Start / Stop
Management Process	10	10:00 / 10:10	_____ / _____
Management Levels	5	10:10 / 10:15	_____ / _____
Supervisory Responsibilities	5	10:15 / 10:20	_____ / _____
Supervisory Roles	1:05	10:20 / 11:25	_____ / _____
Knowledge and Skills for Supervision	20	11:25 / 11:45	_____ / _____
Review and Preview	5	11:45 / 11:50	_____ / _____
Lunch	60	11:50 / 12:50	_____ / _____

4. **Becoming a Supervisor**	**Minutes** **2 hrs. 30**	**Start/Stop** **12:50 / 3:20**	**Actual** **Start / Stop**
Review and Preview	5	12:50 / 12:55	_____ / _____
Challenges Facing New Supervisors	55	12:55 / 1:50	_____ / _____
Skill Practice	35	1:50 / 2:25	_____ / _____
Break	15	2:25 / 2:40	_____ / _____
Video/Film (optional)	40	2:40 / 3:20	_____ / _____

5. **Building a Support Network**	**Minutes** **55**	**Start/Stop** **3:20 / 4:15**	**Actual** **Start / Stop**
Treasure Hunt	30	3:20 / 3:50	_____ / _____
Workshop Summary	5	3:50 / 3:55	_____ / _____
Evaluations	20	3:55 / 4:15	_____ / _____
Total (including two fifteen-minute breaks)	**7.25** **hours**		

Getting Ready

Materials Needed

These are the materials recommended for the one-day supervision training workshop. Masters for the materials are found on the pages indicated. Unless otherwise noted:

- For overhead transparencies, you will need one transparency each.

- For other items, you will need one per participant, plus a few spares.

Overhead Transparencies

☐ Management Process (p. 214).

☐ Management Levels (p. 215).

☐ Supervisory Responsibilities (p. 216).

☐ Supervisory Roles (p. 217).

☐ Supervisory Job Knowledge (p. 218).

☐ Management Skills (p. 219).

☐ Challenges Facing New Supervisors (p. 220).

☐ Round-Robin Skill-Practice (p. 223).

Handouts

☐ The Basics of Supervision (p. 124).

☐ High-Performance Management versus Low-Octane Management (pp. 14-15).

☐ Management Levels (pp. 125-126).

☐ Supervisory Roles (p. 127).

☐ Supervisory Job Knowledge (p. 218).

☐ Management Skills (p. 219).

☐ Challenges Facing New Supervisors (p. 220).

Learning Activities

☐ Get-Acquainted Treasure Hunt, one copy per person, plus 5 prizes (pp. 137).

☐ He's Sinking Fast (p. 141).

☐ Delivering Unpopular News (p. 145).

☐ Preserving the Friendship (p. 148).

☐ Skill-Practice Observer Checklist, three copies per participant (p. 154).

☐ Ignoring the Chain of Command (p. 159).

Tools and Assessments

☐ Supervisory Roles Assessment (pp. 182-183)

☐ Program Evaluation (p. 212).

Special Materials

☐ A film or video is recommended, but optional. If you use this option, select one of the 20- to 30-minute titles listed under the heading " Supervision" in the film/video section of the Appendix.

☐ Five prizes for the winners of the Treasure Hunt activity.

Notes

- _____
- _____
- _____
- _____
- _____
- _____
- _____
- _____
- _____
- _____
- _____
- _____
- _____
- _____
- _____
- _____
- _____

Tailoring Tips

To tailor the workshop to your particular group, do the following:

- For ease in distributing and referring to materials in class, create a handout packet with numbered pages. Bind or staple the packet.

- Design a custom cover with the name of the sponsoring organization, date, and place of the workshop, and print it on heavy paper (cover stock).

- Distribute the packet when you begin the workshop and refer participants to appropriate pages throughout the day.

The suggested order for the materials is:

1. *High-Performance Management versus Low-Octane Management* (pp. 14-15).

2. *Basics of Supervision* (p. 124).

3. *Management Levels* (pp. 125-126).

4. *Supervisory Roles* (p. 127).

5. *Supervisory Roles Assessment* (pp. 182-183).

6. *Supervisory Job Knowledge* (p. 218).

7. *Management Skills* (p. 219).

8. *Challenges Facing New Supervisors* (p. 220).

9. *He's Sinking Fast* (p. 141).

10. *Delivering Unpopular News* (p. 145).

11. *Preserving the Friendship* (p. 148).

12. *Ignoring the Chain of Command* (p. 159).

13. *Skill-Practice: Observer Checklist,* three copies per participant (p. 154).

14. *Get-Acquainted Treasure Hunt* (p. 137).

15. *Program Evaluation* (p. 212).

Things to Do

Prior to conducting the workshop, do the following:

☑ **Prepare materials.**

Before you present the workshop, photocopy the workshop agenda and script. Write your planned start/stop times and anecdotal material on the photocopy.

☑ **Inquire about special needs.**

Meet with the director of training and several of the individuals enrolled in the course to learn about any special needs, internal issues, and the experience level of participants.

☑ **Develop relevant examples.**

Develop examples that are relevant to the industry or enterprise.

☑ **Encourage management participation.**

Invite a middle or top manager to kick off the workshop and emphasize the important role supervisors play.

Training Plan

1. Workshop Overview (45 min.)

Purpose   The purpose of this module is to welcome participants, address housekeeping matters, present an overview of the day's program, and conduct participant introductions.

Objectives   As a result of this module, participants will be able to:

- Describe the workshop objectives.
- List the key topics that will be covered in the workshop.
- Get acquainted with other participants.
- Build their personal network.

Workshop Agenda

1. Workshop Overview	Minutes 45	Start/Stop 8:00 / 8:45	Actual Start / Stop
Welcome	5	8:00 / 8:05	_____ / _____
Workshop Overview	5	8:05 / 8:10	_____ / _____
Paired Participant Introductions	35	8:10 / 8:45	_____ / _____

FACILITATOR COMMENTARY

00: 05   **Welcome**

 WELCOME participants to this workshop.

INTRODUCE yourself and give a brief summary of your qualifications and background.

 TELL participants to write their names on the name cards at their places.

 REVIEW the following housekeeping details:

- Workshop length.
- Anticipated break and lunch times.
- Location of rest rooms, telephones, vending machines, snack and smoking areas, and fire exits.

00:05   **Workshop Overview**

          INTRODUCE the workshop.

- Supervisors are on the front lines, interacting moment by moment with employees to accomplish the enterprise's work. Each day the supervisor's job becomes more challenging as enterprises strive to maintain the high performance levels essential to survival in a fiercely competitive global economy.

- Today we'll discuss why high-performance supervision is vital to organizational health in the new work world.

- Our key topics are:

  - High-performance supervision.

  - The basics of supervision.

  - Making the transition from operating employee to supervisor.

  - Building a support network.

- As a result of participating in this workshop, you'll be able to:

  - Describe the positive effects of high-performance supervision on the enterprise.

  - Describe the four-step supervision process.

  - Describe three management levels.

  - Describe seven basic supervisory responsibilities.

  - Identify roles that supervisors play in different situations.

  - Develop an action plan that addresses the differences between how participants view their roles and the roles others expect them to play.

  - Name four areas of core knowledge needed by supervisors.

  - List three types of skills supervisors need.

  - Describe five challenges faced by new supervisors.

  - Develop strategies for dealing with these challenges.

  - Anticipate problems and address them proactively.

  - Build a support network with other participants.

PAIRED EXERCISE

00:35   **Paired Participant Introductions**

MAKE these comments:

- Let's get to know each other through a process of paired introductions. Find someone you don't know or someone you would like to know better. You'll each have two minutes to interview the other person. Be prepared to introduce the other person to the entire class. During your interview, find out:

  - Name.

  - Organizational unit.

  - How long has the person been in supervision?

  - How many people does the person supervise?

  - Which of the workshop objectives is the person most interested in?

  - One interesting fact about the person (hobby, number of grandchildren, travels, etc.).

- You'll have a total of six minutes—two minutes to find a partner, and two minutes for each interview. Find a partner and start your interviews.

CALL time.

BEGIN the introductions.

POST on a flipchart each participant's name and the workshop objective in which he or she is most interested. Then, tape the chart to the wall so you can refer to it.

FACILITATOR COMMENTARY

MAKE summary points about participants' workshop objectives.

Notes

- _____
- _____
- _____
- _____
- _____
- _____
- _____

2. High-Performance Supervision (1 hr. 15 min.)

Purpose
The purpose of this module is to contrast the healthy results of high-performance supervision with the costly consequences of low-octane supervision, thereby underscoring how vitally important effective supervision is to the enterprise.

Objectives
Upon completion of this segment, participants will be able to:

- Describe the effects of high-performance supervision on the enterprise.

- Describe the effects of low-octane supervision on the enterprise.

- Recognize how important their efforts are to the success of the enterprise where they work.

Workshop Agenda

2. High-Performance Supervision	Minutes 1 hr. 15	Start/Stop 8:45 / 10:00	Actual Start / Stop
High-Performance Supervision versus Low-Octane Supervision	60	8:45 / 9:45	_____ / _____
Break	15	9:45 / 10:00	_____ / _____

FACILITATOR COMMENTARY

01:00

High-Performance Supervision versus Low-Octane Supervision

MAKE these comments:

- It takes high-performance supervision to create high-performance enterprises—the leading edge, world-class organizations that compete successfully in the global economy. At the other end of a continuum, there are low-octane enterprises—the ones that are just sputtering along or coasting downhill.

- On a piece of paper, list three results of high-performance supervision, for example, commitment to a shared vision, high morale, or excellent safety record.

- List three results of low-octane supervision, for example, confusion about goals, political maneuvering.

GROUP ACTIVITY

 ASSIGN participants to groups of five or six people.

 MAKE these comments:

- In your groups, discuss your individual answers. Create two lists, one containing the results of high-performance supervision, and the other, the results of low-octane supervision. I'll distribute flipchart paper, felt-tip pens, and masking tape. Write your group lists on the paper and tape it on the wall. Appoint a spokesperson to explain your chart to the entire class. You have ten minutes to compare your answers, develop your group lists, and create your charts.

 HAVE each group post its flipchart and give its presentation.

 DISTRIBUTE the handout, *High-Performance Management versus Low-Octane Management* (p. 15).

FACILITATOR COMMENTARY

 MAKE this comment:

- This handout contrasts the results of high-performance and low-octane management. Take two minutes to read it.

 ASK for and *ANSWER* any questions.

 MAKE these summary points about the importance of high-performance supervision:

- High performance is essential to survival in a fiercely competitive global economy.

- Most enterprises are in the middle of the continuum between high-performance and low-octane management.

- High-performance supervision is a major factor in building high-performance organizations.

- Your supervision skills make a significant difference.

00:15   **Break**

---

3. The Basics of Supervision
(1 hr. 50 min.)

Purpose

The purpose of this module is to describe the basic functions, responsibilities, and roles of the supervisor, as well as the knowledge and skills required to be an effective supervisor.

Objectives

As a result of this module, participants will be able to:

- Describe the four-step supervision process.

- Describe three management levels.

- Describe seven basic supervisory responsibilities.

- Identify roles that supervisors play in different situations.

- Develop an action plan that addresses the differences in how the participant views his or her roles and the roles others expect the supervisor to play.

- Name four areas of core knowledge needed by supervisors.

- List three types of skills supervisors need.

Workshop Agenda

3. The Basics of Supervision	Minutes 1 hr. 50	Start/Stop 10:00 / 11:50	Actual Start / Stop
Management Process	10	10:00 / 10:10	_____ / _____
Management Levels	5	10:10 / 10:15	_____ / _____
Supervisory Responsibilities	5	10:15 / 10:20	_____ / _____
Supervisory Roles	1:05	10:20 / 11:25	_____ / _____
Knowledge and Skills for Supervision	20	11:25 / 11:45	_____ / _____
Review and Preview	5	11:45 / 11:50	_____ / _____
Lunch	60	11:50 / 12:50	_____ / _____

FACILITATOR COMMENTARY

Management Process

 DISTRIBUTE the handout, *Basics of Supervision* (p. 124).

 MAKE these comments:

- The next segment of our workshop covers the basics of supervision.

- Supervisors occupy the first rung on the management ladder.

 REFER to the handout titled *Basics of Supervision*.

- Supervisors focus the efforts of operating (nonmanagerial) employees to accomplish the enterprise's goals.

 SHOW the overhead transparency titled *Management Process*, (p. 214).

 MAKE these comments:

- Management is a four-step process of planning, organizing, leading, and controlling an enterprise's resources to achieve its mission and objectives.

- Planning is the process of envisioning the future, setting goals, identifying actions to achieve the goals, establishing target dates for completing the actions, and describing measures of success.

- In the management process, the organizing function follows the planning function. Supervisors perform the organizing function when they divide work into specific tasks, develop work schedules, decide where work will be performed, decide what equipment and methods will be used, and delegate assignments.

- Leading is the process of influencing other people to follow in the achievement of a common goal.

- Controlling involves setting standards, measuring performance against those standards, rewarding desired behaviors and taking corrective action when necessary.

- These four steps are interdependent functions in a dynamic cycle that can be interrupted at any point.

GROUP DISCUSSION

ASK these questions and look for answers that make the following points:

- What does it mean when we say the four steps are interdependent?

    – Dependent upon each other, mutually related, they influence each other.

- What is a dynamic cycle?

    – A cycle is a regularly repeated sequence of steps. Planning, organizing, leading, and controlling occur in a sequence.

    – A dynamic cycle is a regularly repeated sequence of steps marked by continuous change or progress. One of the reasons that the cycle is dynamic is because the four functions are interdependent. That is, what happens at one stage of the process influences the other stages.

MAKE the following points:

- For example, during the planning phase of a project, controls such as target dates are established. For any number of reasons, some outside the team's control, the schedule can slip, making revisions to the plan and target dates necessary.

- Managers at every level perform the four-step process of planning, organizing, leading, and controlling to achieve the enterprise's mission and objectives. What differs at each level is the focus managers take as they perform their functions. Top management takes a long-term strategic focus, middle management an intermediate focus, and first-line supervisors a near-term operational focus.

- The principles of management apply to any organization: for-profit and not-for-profit, public sector and private, small and large, manufacturing and service.

FACILITATOR COMMENTARY

00:05   **Management Levels**

 SHOW the overhead transparency titled *Management Levels*, (p. 215).

 MAKE these comments:

- Most organizations have three broad management levels: executive or top management, middle management, and first-line supervision. In large organizations, each level can have several sublevels within it. Take three minutes to read the handout titled *Management Levels*.

 DISTRIBUTE copies of handout titled *Management Levels*, (pp. 125-126).

 ASK for and *ANSWER* any questions.

00:05   **Supervisory Responsibilities**

 MAKE these comments:

In addition to performing the management functions of planning, organizing, leading, and controlling, supervisors have seven basic responsibilities.

1. **Production.**

   Delivering the product or service with the available resources.

2. **Morale.**

   Stimulating a positive work attitude on the part of employees.

3. **Quality.**

   Stimulating quality-consciousness and job pride in the work-force.

4. **Costs.**

   Contributing to the enterprise's profitability by cost control and cost reduction.

5. **Methods.**

   Seeking easier and better ways of doing work.

6. **Training.**

   Teaching employees how to perform their jobs and stay current with changing technology.

7. **Safety.**

   Minimizing risks and hazards in the work area.

MAKE the following points:

- Each of these responsibilities requires supervisory attention. Their relative importance may change from time to time, but none can be overlooked.

- These responsibilities are interrelated. Take production for example. Overemphasis on production can hurt morale. Conversely, trying to keep everyone happy can lead to country-club style management and diminished productivity. Or consider the relationship between quality and cost. Quality can drive costs up; however, overzealous cost-cutting can result in poor-quality goods reaching the marketplace.

GROUP DISCUSSION

01:05

Supervisory Roles

 ASK these questions and look for answers like the following:

- So far, we've said that the supervision process involved four functions. What are those four functions?

  - Planning, organizing, leading, and controlling.

- We've said that supervisors have seven basic responsibilities. What are those responsibilities?

  - Production, morale, quality, costs, methods, training, and safety.

 MAKE this comment:

- Well, there's more. Supervisors also assume a variety of roles each day.

 ASK this question and look for answers like the following:

- What's a role?

  - A role is a character that the supervisor assumes in a particular situation, much like an actor plays a role in a film.

 MAKE these comments:

- While assuming a role, the supervisor must mentally put on the costume that fits the role. For instance, when a supervisor deals with a conflict between two employees, he or she might be mentally wearing a referee's striped shirt and throwing a yellow handkerchief on the field of play.

- Here are some typical roles:

 SHOW the overhead transparency titled *Supervisory Roles* (p. 217).

ASK this question and look for answers like the following:

* What costumes would supervisors mentally wear when they assume the roles listed on the transparency?

    – Team captain—football uniform.

    – Hunter—hunting jacket.

    – Gladiator—suit of armor and shield.

    – Fortune teller—crystal ball.

DISTRIBUTE copies of *Supervisory Roles* (p. 127).

ASK this question:

* Take two minutes to review this list of supervisory roles. What other roles can you add?

DISTRIBUTE copies of the *Supervisory Roles Assessment*, (pp. 182-185).

INDIVIDUAL ACTIVITY

 MAKE these comments to introduce the assessment:

* Next you're going to complete a *Supervisory Roles Assessment*. The assessment has three parts:

    – Part I gives you practice identifying supervisory roles.

    – Part II asks you to apply your general knowledge about supervisory roles to your personal situation by describing the roles that you play and the roles that others expect you to play.

    – In Part III, *Action Planning*, you analyze the similarities and differences between the roles you play and the roles others expect you to play. Then you develop an action plan to address the differences.

* You'll have four minutes to complete Part I of the assessment. Begin now.

CALL time on the individual activity.

GROUP DISCUSSION

 ASSIGN participants to pairs or trios to discuss their answers to Part I, Column B of the worksheet.

MAKE this comment:

- You have five minutes to compare your answers to Part I of the *Supervisory Roles Assessment.*

 CALL time on the small group discussion.

 ASK for volunteers to share their answers.

LOOK for answers that are similar to those provided in the facilitator's version of the *Supervisory Roles Assessment.*

INDIVIDUAL ACTIVITY

 MAKE these comments:

- Next, you're going to work on your own again. Complete Part II of the assessment. Then, select one of the situations you described in Part II for action planning in Part III. With respect to that one situation only, answer Part III, questions 1 through 4, and complete the action planning and target dates columns of the action planning form. You have eight minutes. Once you've written your individual action plans, you'll discuss them in small groups.

 CALL time on the individual activity.

GROUP ACTIVITY

 ASSIGN participants to pairs or trios to discuss their answers to Parts II and III of the worksheet.

MAKE this comment:

- You have eight minutes to compare your answers to Parts II and III of the *Supervisory Roles Assessment.*

CALL time on the small group discussion.

ASK for volunteers to share their answers.

ASK these questions and look for answers like the following:

- When your roles differ from the expectations of others, how does this affect interpersonal relationships and productivity?

  – Causes confusion, disappointment, frustration, conflict, resentment.

  – Productivity decreases.

- What steps can you take to create clarity about roles?

  – Discuss differences in perception.

  – Engage in joint problem solving.

  – Clarify and renegotiate roles.

FACILITATOR COMMENTARY

 MAKE the following summary points about supervisory roles:

- A role is a character that a supervisor assumes, much like an actor plays a role in a film.

- Supervisors play many roles every day.

- When the roles supervisors play differ from the expectations others have of them, confusion can result. This confusion can lead to poor interpersonal relationships and loss of productivity.

- To clarify roles:

  – Discuss differences in perception.

  – Engage in joint problem solving.

  – Renegotiate roles.

00:20 **Knowledge and Skills for Supervision**

 MAKE these comments:

- So far, we've said that supervisors perform four functions: planning, organizing, leading, and controlling.

- We've listed seven basic responsibilities: production, morale, quality, costs, methods, training, and safety. Each of those responsibilities requires supervisory attention. You can't neglect any of them.

- And, we've said supervisors assume a variety of roles each day.

- Well, it's a tall order to be juggling four functions, seven responsibilities, and a whole repertoire of roles. So the next topic we're going to explore is "Knowledge and Skills Required for Supervision."

REVIEW the definitions of knowledge and skill.

- Knowledge is awareness or comprehension acquired by experience or study.
- A skill is a proficiency at performing a task.

SHOW and ***DISTRIBUTE*** the overhead transparency titled *Supervisory Job Knowledge* (p. 218).

REFER to the appropriate point on the transparency and ***MAKE*** these comments:

- Supervisors need the following core knowledge:
  1. Solid technical knowledge about work methods and equipment.
  2. Knowledge of how to manage resources, particularly human resources.

GROUP DISCUSSION

ASK this question and look for answers like the following:

- In addition to human resources, what other resources do supervisors manage?
  - Funds, facilities, equipment, tools, supplies, machinery, time.

REVIEW point three on the transparency:

  3. A broad knowledge-base about their enterprise.

ASK this question and look for answers like the following:

- What do supervisors need to know about their enterprise?
  - Mission, culture, values.
  - Key employees, customers, suppliers, competitors.
  - Administrative procedures, policies, rules.
  - Information and records system.

REFER to point four on the transparency:

  4. Knowledge of their industry.

ASK this question and look for answers like the following:

- What do supervisors need to know about their industry?
  - Where it's headed.
  - Who the industry leaders are and why.
  - Pace of change.

FACILITATOR COMMENTARY

 SHOW and *DISTRIBUTE* the overhead transparency titled *Management Skills* (p. 219).

 MAKE these comments:

- Three management skills or proficiencies are essential to successful performance of the planning, organizing, leading, and controlling functions:

  1. **Human relations skills.**

     Human relations skills are partly knowledge-based and partly intuitive. They rest on an understanding of human behavior, interpersonal communication skills, and personal style flexibility.

  2. **Technical skills or job know-how.**

     Technical skills are proficiencies at using specific methods, techniques, tools, equipment, or software. Examples include operating a drill press, reading blueprints, using word processing software or electronic spreadsheets, dispensing prescriptions, or performing library research or database searches. Usually technical skills count most at the supervisory level, because supervisors give direction to operating employees.

  3. **Conceptual skills.**

     Conceptual skills allow managers to comprehend abstract or general ideas and apply them to specific situations, as well as to see underlying patterns in seemingly unrelated events. Conceptual skills are essential for planning, problem solving, decision making, writing, and public speaking.

00:05   **Review and Preview**

 SUMMARIZE the morning session.

MAKE these comments:

- This afternoon, we will cover the challenges new supervisors face.

- Right now, we're going to take a lunch break. The workshop will resume promptly at (give the time).

01:00   **Lunch**

4. Becoming a Supervisor (2 hrs. 30 min.)

Purpose   The purpose of this module is to describe challenges new supervisors face as they make the transition from operating employee to a member of the management ranks, and to give participants skill practice in addressing the challenges.

Objectives   As a result of this module, participants will be able to:

- Describe five challenges faced by new supervisors.

- Develop strategies for dealing with these challenges.

- Anticipate problems and address them proactively.

Workshop Agenda

4. Becoming a Supervisor	Minutes 2 hrs. 30	Start/Stop 12:50 / 3:20	Actual Start / Stop
Review and Preview	5	12:50 / 12:55	_____ / _____
Challenges Facing New Supervisors	55	12:55 / 1:50	_____ / _____
Skill Practice	35	1:50 / 2:25	_____ / _____
Break	15	2:25 / 2:40	_____ / _____
Video/Film (optional)	40	2:40 / 3:20	_____ / _____

FACILITATOR COMMENTARY

00:05

Review and Preview

WELCOME participants back from lunch.

ASK these questions and look for answers like the following:

- Does anyone have any questions or comments about the material we covered this morning?

- What were the key topics we covered this morning?

  – High-performance supervision, functions of the supervisor, supervisory responsibilities, roles, levels of management, and knowledge and skills required for supervision.

MAKE this comment:

- This afternoon, we will cover how to make the transition from operating employee to supervisor.

00:55   **Challenges Facing New Supervisors**

SHOW and *DISTRIBUTE* the overhead transparency titled *Challenges Facing New Supervisors* (p. 220).

MAKE these comments:

- Often operating employees are not properly prepared to become supervisors. After the excitement over the promotion fades, a new supervisor faces the following challenges:

    – **Lack of job preparation.**

    A new supervisor may not know much about managing resources and accomplishing work through others.

    – **Change in roles from operating employee to supervisor.**

    The new supervisor must take on the role of leader and administrator, and give up the role of skilled worker and individual contributor. The new supervisor has to establish authority over the work unit without overcontrolling. The supervisor must change from doer to delegator.

    – **Changes in relationships.**

    When recently promoted supervisors have former coworkers reporting to them, the relationships change.

    – **Changes in perspective.**

    Instead of concentrating on how to fulfill the duties of one job, new supervisors must consider how to focus the unit's efforts in support of the enterprise's goals.

    – **Lack of a support system.**

    Often, new supervisors don't know where to turn for help during their challenging career transition.

DISTRIBUTE copies of the learning activities, *He's Sinking Fast* (p. 141); *Delivering Unpopular News* (p. 145); *Preserving the Friendship* (p. 148); *Skill-Practice: Observer Checklist* (p. 154); and *Ignoring the Chain of Command* (p. 159).

INDIVIDUAL ACTIVITY

MAKE these comments:

- To take a closer look at challenges new supervisors face and to develop strategies to address those situations, we're going to study four case situations involving new supervisors. The cases are in the handout packet that you have just received. As individuals, read the four cases. Write your answers to the questions that accompany each case in the space provided on the handout. You have ten minutes.

GROUP ACTIVITY

 ASSIGN participants to teams of three people.

 MAKE this comment:

- Discuss your individual answers to the case study questions, and develop team answers to the questions. Be prepared to share your team responses with the entire class. You have twenty minutes; that's five minutes per case. Appoint a member of the group to serve as timekeeper.

 CALL time when twenty minutes have elapsed.

 ASK for volunteers to present their team's answers to the discussion questions that accompany the case studies.

LOOK for answers that make the points provided in the Facilitator's Copy of the case studies in Chapter 8, *Learning Activities*.

FACILITATOR COMMENTARY

 MAKE these summary points about the transition from operating employee to supervisor:

- Making the transition from operating employee to supervisor is challenging. Here are some steps new supervisors can take:
  - Recognize and accept the fact that your role has changed. You must now take a management perspective.
  - Strike a balance between overcontrol and undercontrol.
  - Develop a support team, including your manager, your peers, and your family.
- Experienced supervisors can help new supervisors navigate the transition by taking the initiative and offering to serve as a resource.

00:35   **Skill Practice**

MAKE these comments:

- It is as important for supervisors to practice their skills in a classroom learning laboratory as it is for an athlete to practice on the playing field. So, the next activity is a skill practice. Three of the cases that we just discussed are the basis of the skill practice:

  - *Delivering Unpopular News*

  - *Preserving the Friendship*

  - *Ignoring the Chain of Command*

- Continue to work in the same trios that you had during the case discussions.

DISTRIBUTE three copies of the *Skill-Practice: Observer Checklist* to each participant (p. 154).

SHOW the overhead transparency titled *Round-Robin Skill-Practice* (p. 223).

MAKE these comments:

- We're going to do a "round-robin" skill practice that runs for three rounds. During Round One, *Delivering Unpopular News*, person A in the trio will be Judy, the supervisor, and person B will be Dan, the employee. Person C is the observer and timekeeper. If there are four in a group, the fourth person serves as an observer, also. You'll have three minutes to practice the meeting between Judy and Dan on the new telephone policy, and three minutes for feedback and discussion on how the skill practice went.

- Observers are to use the checklist as a guide for your observation and for the feedback you give to the "supervisor" and "employee."

- In Round Two, *Preserving the Friendship*, person B is Barry, the supervisor. Person C is Robert, the employee. Person A is the observer.

- In Round Three, *Ignoring the Chain of Command*, person C is Carla, the supervisor. Person A is Phil, the employee. Person B is the observer.

- You have six minutes per round, or eighteen minutes total for the three rounds of skill practice. After the practice, I'm going to ask each trio to give us one insight they gained from the skill-practice.

ASK for and *ANSWER* any questions.

GROUP ACTIVITY

 BEGIN the skill practice.

 CALL time on the skill practice.

 ASK each trio for one insight.

FACILITATOR COMMENTARY

 MAKE the following summary points about the skill practice:

- You've just had practice using communication, negotiation, conflict-management, and problem-solving skills during this exercise. In addition, you've had an opportunity to observe others using these skills and learn from your observations.

- Let's take a 15-minute break.

00:15   **Break**

00:40   **Video/Film (Optional)**

 MAKE these comments:

- Now we're going to watch a video/film that shows common mistakes new supervisors make and illustrates behaviors used by successful supervisors. The video is also a good review for experienced supervisors, because no matter how experienced, they can fall into the same traps as new supervisors. The title of the film is: (Select one of the 20- to 30-minute films listed under the heading "Supervision" in the film/video section of the Appendix (pp. 231-233) or comparable.)

INTRODUCE the video and its characters.

 SHOW the video.

 ASK this question:

- What ideas did you learn from the video that you can apply on the job?

 MAKE a summary statement of the key ideas from the video.

5. Building a Support Network (55 min.)

Purpose   The purpose of this module is to emphasize the importance of building a support network, and to give participants the opportunity to network during the workshop.

Objectives   As a result of this module, participants will be able to:

- Network with fifteen other participants.

- Recognize the value of networking to their effectiveness as supervisors.

Workshop Agenda

5. Building a Support Network	Minutes 55	Start/Stop 3:20 / 4:15	Actual Start / Stop
Treasure Hunt	30	3:20 / 3:50	_____ / _____
Workshop Summary	5	3:50 / 3:55	_____ / _____
Evaluations	20	3:55 / 4:15	_____ / _____
Total (including two fifteen-minute breaks)	**7.25 hours**		

FACILITATOR COMMENTARY

00:30   **Treasure Hunt**

MAKE these comments:

- Building a network is an important by-product of workshops. Each person in your network is a treasure of information, help, and support. Our next activity is a treasure hunt that provides an opportunity to expand your network.

GROUP ACTIVITY

DISTRIBUTE the Learning Activity titled *Get-Acquainted Treasure Hunt* (p. 137).

REFER to the facilitator's instructions that accompany the *Get-Acquainted Treasure Hunt* for directions (p. 136).

MAKE the following comments to conclude the activity:

- I encourage you to stay in touch with the people you have met in this workshop. You can be an excellent source of information, resources, and encouragement for each other. Supervision is a challenging job, and the support network you build now will serve you well for years to come.

FACILITATOR COMMENTARY

00:05

Workshop Summary

MAKE these comments:

- The key topics that we've covered today in our workshop on High-Performance Supervision are:

  - We have contrasted the healthy results of high-performance supervision with the costly consequences of low-octane supervision.

  - We have covered the basics of supervision, including functions, responsibilities, roles, required knowledge and skills.

  - We have examined the challenges that new supervisors face when they move from operating employee to supervisor.

  - You have written an action plan to address a situation where you and a coworker have differing role expectations.

  - You practiced your communication, negotiation, conflict-management, and problem-solving skills during our skill practice this afternoon.

  - You added to your support network by meeting and exchanging ideas with your classmates here today.

- High-performance supervision is crucial to the success of your organization. Today's competition is too keen for low-octane management. So, when you return to the workplace, apply the skills and use the information you gained here.

- You've been an outstanding group. Thank you for your participation. Good luck in your careers as supervisors.

INDIVIDUAL ACTIVITY

00:20

Evaluations

- We'd appreciate some feedback from each of you about the workshop. I'm going to distribute an evaluation form. Please complete it now. Afterward, place the form on the table by the door, and you are free to leave. Again, thank you and good luck.

DISTRIBUTE the *Program Evaluation* (p. 212).

Chapter Five

Half-Day Supervision Workshop

This chapter contains the training plan for your half-day supervision workshop—ready to go "as is" or to be tailored to meet your needs. The chapter is divided into three parts:

- Workshop Agenda.

- Getting Ready.

- Training Plan.

"PLANNING AND ORGANIZING WORK"

This workshop is designed for new or experienced supervisors. The purpose is to provide background on and techniques for planning, organizing, and delegating. In addition, the workshop participants practice skills presented in the workshop and develop plans for applying those skills at work. When participants have completed this session, they will be able to:

- Identify tasks to be performed.

- Develop an action plan to achieve a balance of supervisory functions.

- Successfully delegate an assignment.

Workshop Agenda

1. Workshop Overview	Minutes 25	Start/Stop 8:00 / 8:25	Actual Start / Stop
Welcome	5	8:00 / 8:05	_____ / _____
Workshop Overview	5	8:05 / 8:10	_____ / _____
Participant Introductions	15	8:10 / 8:25	_____ / _____

2. Planning	Minutes 1 hr. 40	Start/Stop 8:25 / 10:05	Actual Start / Stop
Overview	5	8:25 / 8:30	_____ / _____
Payoffs of Planning	30	8:30 / 9:00	_____ / _____
Planning Survey	30	9:00 / 9:30	_____ / _____
Developing and Implementing a Plan	15	9:30 / 9:45	_____ / _____
Module Summary	5	9:45 / 9:50	_____ / _____
Break	15	9:50 / 10:05	

3. Organizing Tasks and People	Minutes 25	Start/Stop 10:05 / 10:30	Actual Start / Stop
Module Overview	5	10:05 / 10:10	_____ / _____
Organizing Survey	15	10:10 / 10:25	_____ / _____
Key Organizing Questions	4	10:25 / 10:29	_____ / _____
Module Summary	1	10:29 / 10:30	_____ / _____

4. **Delegating**	Minutes 1 hr. 15	Start/Stop 10:30 / 11:45	Actual Start / Stop
Module Overview	5	10:30 / 10:35	_____ / _____
Benefits of Delegating	5	10:35 / 10:40	_____ / _____
Barriers to Delegating	5	10:40 / 10:45	_____ / _____
Delegation Process	12	10:45 / 10:57	_____ / _____
Delegation Planning	8	10:57 / 11:05	_____ / _____
Delegation Skill-Practice	25	11:05 / 11:30	_____ / _____
Module Summary	1	11:30 / 11:31	_____ / _____
Workshop Summary	4	11:31 / 11:35	_____ / _____
Workshop Evaluations	10	11:35 / 11:45	_____ / _____
Total (including one fifteen-minute break)	**3.75 hours**		

Getting Ready

Materials Needed

These are the materials that are recommended for the half-day Planning and Organizing workshop. Page references indicate where masters for the materials are found elsewhere in this book. Unless otherwise noted:

- For overhead transparencies, you will need one transparency each.

- For other items, you will need one per participant, plus a few spares.

Overhead Transparencies

☐ Implementing a Plan (p. 224).

☐ Delegation Process (p. 221).

☐ Round-Robin Skill-Practice (p. 223).

Handouts

☐ Implementing a Plan (p. 224).

☐ Key Organizing Questions (p. 129).

☐ What Is Delegation? (p. 130).

☐ Delegation Process (p. 221).

☐ Creating Goals and Objectives (p. 128).

Learning Activities

☐ Delegation Planning Worksheet (p. 168).

☐ Delegation Skill-Practice: Observer Checklist,
3 copies per participant (p. 169).

Tools and Assessments

☐ Planning Survey (pp. 188-189).

☐ Organizing Survey (pp. 196-197).

☐ Program Evaluation (p. 212).

Special Materials

☐ Several blank sheets of paper for each participant. These may be bound into the back of the participants' handout packets. Participants will use these during the individual activity, Payoffs of Planning.

Notes

- _____
- _____
- _____
- _____
- _____
- _____
- _____
- _____
- _____
- _____
- _____
- _____
- _____
- _____
- _____
- _____
- _____
- _____
- _____
- _____
- _____
- _____

Tailoring Tips

To tailor the workshop to your particular group, do the following:

- For ease in distributing and referring to materials in class, create a numbered handout packet. Bind or staple the packet.

- Design a custom cover with the name of the sponsoring organization, date, and place of the workshop, and print it on heavy paper (cover stock).

- Distribute the packet when you begin the workshop and refer participants to appropriate pages throughout the day.

The suggested order for the materials is:

1. *Planning Survey* (pp. 188-189).

2. *Implementing a Plan* (p. 224).

3. *Organizing Survey* (pp. 196-197).

4. *Key Organizing Questions* (p. 129).

5. *What Is Delegation?* (p. 130).

6. *Delegation Process* (p. 221).

7. *Delegation Planning Worksheet* (p. 168).

8. *Delegation Skill-Practice: Observer Checklist*, three copies per participant (p. 169).

9. *Program Evaluation* (p. 212).

Customization Options

To create a customized half-day workshop, try the following:

- **A Half-Day Planning Workshop**

  To create a half-day workshop on planning, deliver Module 1, *Workshop Overview* (pp. 90-92) (deleting the references to organizing) and Module 2, *Planning* (pp. 93-99) of the half-day workshop on Planning and Organizing Work that follows, and then use the learning activity, *Going Through the Work Orders* (pp. 160-166).

- **A Half-Day Delegation Workshop**

  To create a half-day workshop on delegation, deliver Module 1, *Workshop Overview* (pp. 90-92) (deleting the references to planning) and Module 3, *Organizing Tasks and People* (pp. 100-102). Then use the learning activity, *Giving Instructions* (pp. 170-174), following the instructions in the One-Hour Training Plan (pp. 117-121). Lastly, present Module 4 on *Delegating* (pp. 103-110), customizing the workshop summary to fit your program.

Things to Do

Prior to conducting the workshop, do the following:

Prepare materials.

Before you present the workshop, photocopy the workshop agenda and script. Write your planned start/stop times and anecdotal material on the photocopy.

Inquire about special needs.

Meet with the director of training and several of the individuals enrolled in the course to learn about any special needs, internal issues, and the experience level of participants.

Develop relevant examples.

Develop examples that are relevant to the industry or enterprise.

Encourage management participation.

Invite a middle or top manager to kick off the workshop and emphasize the important role that supervisors play.

Training Plan

1. Workshop Overview (25 min.)

Purpose   The purpose of this module is to welcome participants, address housekeeping matters, present an overview of the half-day program, and conduct participant introductions.

Objectives   As a result of this module, participants will be able to:

- Describe the workshop objectives.

- List the key topics that will be covered in the workshop.

- Get acquainted with other participants.

Workshop Agenda

1. Workshop Overview	Minutes 25	Start/Stop 8:00 / 8:25	Actual Start / Stop
Welcome	5	8:00 / 8:05	_____ / _____
Workshop Overview	5	8:05 / 8:10	_____ / _____
Participant Introductions	15	8:10 / 8:25	_____ / _____

FACILITATOR COMMENTARY

00:05   **Welcome**

 WELCOME participants to this workshop on planning and organizing work.

INTRODUCE yourself and give a brief summary of your qualifications and background.

 TELL participants to write their names on the name cards at their places.

 REVIEW the following housekeeping details:

- Workshop length.

- Anticipated break time.

- Location of restrooms, telephones, vending machines, snack and smoking areas, and fire exits.

00:05   **Workshop Overview**

    INTRODUCE the workshop.

- Management is a four-step process of planning, organizing, leading, and controlling an enterprise's resources to achieve its mission and objectives. In this workshop, we will focus on the planning and organizing functions of the four-step process.

- Planning is the process of envisioning the future, setting goals, identifying actions to achieve the goals, establishing target dates for completing the actions, and describing measures of success.

- The organizing function follows the planning function. Supervisors perform the organizing function when they divide work into specific tasks, set work schedules, decide where work will be performed, decide what methods will be used, and delegate assignments. Because delegation is such an important part of the organizing function, this workshop places special emphasis on delegation.

Objectives

- As a result of participating in this workshop, you'll be able to:

  - Identify planning tasks that you perform.

  - Assess whether you spend the right amount of time on planning tasks.

  - Create an action plan to achieve the appropriate balance between planning and other supervisory functions.

  - Identify organizing tasks that you perform.

  - Assess whether you spend the right amount of time on organizing tasks.

  - Develop an action plan to achieve the appropriate balance between organizing and other supervisory functions.

  - Plan to delegate an assignment when at work.

  - Practice delegating the planned assignment.

GROUP ACTIVITY

00:15   **Participant Introductions**

MAKE these comments:

- Introduce yourselves to the others at your table by providing the following information:
    - Name.
    - Organizational unit.
    - How long you have been in supervision.
    - How many people you supervise.
    - Which of the workshop key topics interest you the most.
- Appoint a group representative to give a one minute summary of your small group discussion by telling us:
    - How long members have been in supervision.
    - What topics interest your group the most.
- You have five minutes.

HAVE groups present their reports.

FACILITATOR COMMENTARY

POST on a flipchart pad topics that interest people the most. Then, tape the charts to the wall so you can refer to them.

MAKE summary points about the high-interest topics.

Notes

- _____
- _____
- _____
- _____
- _____
- _____
- _____
- _____
- _____
- _____
- _____

2. Planning (1 hr. 40 min.)

Purpose

The purpose of this module is to give supervisors an overview of the planning function. In addition, the module allows supervisors to identify planning tasks that they perform, and to develop an action plan to achieve an appropriate balance between planning and other supervisory functions. Finally, supervisors will learn a step-by-step method for developing and implementing a plan.

Objectives

As a result of this module, participants will be able to:

- Identify planning tasks they perform.

- Assess whether they spend the right amount of time on planning tasks.

- Create an action plan to achieve the appropriate balance between planning and other supervisory functions.

- Describe a seven-step method for developing and implementing plans.

Workshop Agenda

2. Planning	Minutes 1 hr. 40	Start/Stop 8:25 / 10:05	Actual Start / Stop
Overview	5	8:25 / 8:30	_____ / _____
Payoffs of Planning	30	8:30 / 9:00	_____ / _____
Planning Survey	30	9:00 / 9:30	_____ / _____
Developing and Implementing a Plan	15	9:30 / 9:45	_____ / _____
Module Summary	5	9:45 / 9:50	_____ / _____
Break	15	9:50 / 10:05	

FACILITATOR COMMENTARY

00:05

Overview

REVIEW module objectives.

MAKE these comments:

- Planning is the process of envisioning the future, setting goals, identifying actions to achieve the goals, establishing target dates for completing the actions, and describing measures of success.

- A plan is a written document which serves as a road map that shows the way to the desired goal or destination.

- As the first function in the supervision process, planning provides a basis for organizing, leading, and controlling. For instance, the plan dictates how work will be *organized*. Supervisors must *lead* in the direction mapped out in the plan. Finally, supervisors *control* using standards of performance described in the plan, such as target dates or quantities.

- Supervisors are planning when they:

  - Create work schedules.

  - Develop the unit's annual budget.

  - Create a vacation schedule.

  - Make plans to obtain materials, tools, and equipment in a timely manner.

  - Establish the preventive maintenance schedule for equipment.

  - Think about where the work unit is going in relation to the enterprise's goals.

  - Develop goals and objectives for the next performance cycle.

  - Build a skilled and balanced work team that will be capable of meeting the work unit's future needs.

00:30

Payoffs of Planning

MAKE these comments:

- On a blank piece of paper list three payoffs of planning; for example, planning ensures that materials and supplies will be available when needed.

- Now list three barriers to planning; for example, we're too busy with day-to-day activities to plan.

GROUP ACTIVITY

 ASSIGN participants to groups of five or six people.

 DISTRIBUTE chart paper, felt-tip pens, and masking tape.

 MAKE these comments:

- In your groups, discuss your individual answers. Create two lists, one containing the payoffs of planning and the other the barriers to planning.

- Write your group lists on the chart paper and tape it on the wall. Appoint a spokesperson to explain your chart to the entire class.

- You have ten minutes to compare your answers, develop your group lists, and create your charts.

 CALL time when ten minutes have passed.

GROUP DISCUSSION

 BEGIN the small group reports.

 LOOK for answers that make the following points:

Payoffs

- Makes it possible to influence the future, instead of reacting to events.

- Increases the likelihood that quality products and services will be delivered on time and within budget.

- Gives a basis for deciding how to allocate limited resources to the most important priorities.

- Contributes to economical use of resources, for example, by avoiding overtime or allowing materials to be purchased at favorable prices.

- Improves communication and coordination.

- Helps the supervisor decide what to delegate and to whom.

- Allows the work team to measure progress using the plan's benchmarks or controls.

- Heightens employee motivation to achieve goals in anticipation of agreed-upon rewards.

- Improves quality when standards described in the plan are met.

- Increases efficiency of operations and productivity.

- Helps the supervisor perform the leading function because the plan provides a destination and a road map.

GROUP DISCUSSION

Barriers

Note: The accompanying parenthetical notes provide the facilitator with possible responses to participants' objections to planning.

- The supervisor and work team don't have time to plan because they are too busy with day-to-day activities. (Planning can increase productivity, because employees have clear priorities, target dates, and the necessary resources.)

- Circumstances change too rapidly to plan. (Planning allows early identification of potential problems or opportunities, making it possible to develop response strategies.)

- Those involved view planning as a waste of time. (In the long run, planning generally saves more time than it takes.)

- Plans become obsolete almost immediately because priorities change. (Planning creates a baseline that can be used to evaluate the relative importance of new or emerging priorities.)

FACILITATOR COMMENTARY

SUMMARIZE the major themes from the group reports.

MAKE this comment:

- When you weigh the payoffs and barriers to planning, remember that when you invest time in planning, you will get a return on that investment. In the long run, planning generally saves more time than it costs.

00:30　　　**Planning Survey**

DISTRIBUTE the *Planning Survey* (pp. 188-189).

MAKE this comment:

- This *Planning Survey* gives you the opportunity to identify planning tasks that you perform, assess whether you spend the right amount of time on these tasks, and list actions that you will take when you return to the workplace to arrive at the appropriate balance between planning and other supervisory functions. Look at your surveys, and we'll review the directions together.

INDIVIDUAL ACTIVITY

REVIEW the *Planning Survey* directions (p. 186-187).

MAKE this comment:

- You have ten minutes to complete the survey and action plan. Begin now.

CALL time when ten minutes have elapsed.

GROUP ACTIVITY

ASSIGN participants to pairs or trios.

MAKE this comment:

- In your teams, discuss the results of your planning surveys and action plans. You have five minutes.

CALL time when five minutes have elapsed.

GROUP DISCUSSION

ASK these questions:

- What activities listed on the survey take up too much of your time and what actions will you take?

- What activities listed on the survey require more time and what actions will you take?

FACILITATOR COMMENTARY

SUMMARIZE the discussion to conclude the activity.

00:15   **Developing and Implementing a Plan**

SHOW the overhead transparency, *Implementing a Plan* (p. 224) and *DISTRIBUTE* copies of the handout, *Creating Goals and Objectives* (p. 128).

FACILITATOR COMMENTARY

 MAKE these comments:

There are seven steps for developing and implementing a plan.

1. **Do homework.**

   Planning requires a clear picture of where the work unit was last year with respect to its key result areas, where it is now, and where it will be next year. To bring this picture into clear focus, you need the following information:

   - Accomplishments.
   - Mission Statement.
   - Management Expectations.
   - External Developments.

2. **Involve the team.**

   Give employees background, describe the unit's key result areas, and seek employees' ideas about unit goals and objectives. Undoubtedly this exercise will generate a surplus of ideas; so, the team will have to narrow the list.

3. **Turn ideas into a written plan.**

   Turn ideas into a written plan with clearly designated action items, responsible individuals identified, and target dates set.

4. **Review the draft plan and gain commitment.**

   Review your draft plan with team members and with your manager. After gaining agreement and commitment, you can create a final version that everyone will be expected to live by for the upcoming year.

5. **Implement the plan.**

   This is when the plan gets turned into action. Distribute the plan at a team meeting to let everyone know that the starting gun has sounded. Also, let people know they will be held accountable for the actions they agreed to implement.

6. **Monitor progress.**

   Regular progress reviews are essential to keeping the project on target. These reviews also serve as an opportune time to provide suggestions, encouragement, and praise. Plans aren't cast in concrete; they can be flexible. There will be times when new circumstances dictate changes in the plan.

7. Reward accomplishments.

Employees deserve to be recognized for a job well done with both monetary rewards and with ceremonies and celebrations. The rewards not only keep high performers motivated, they provide incentives and role models for others as well.

 ASK for and *ANSWER* any questions.

00:05   **Module Summary**

 MAKE these summary points about planning:

- Planning makes it possible to influence the future rather than react to events.

- Supervisors implement operational plans—plans that specify what work will be performed in their immediate work units, along with starting and completion dates.

- Plans must be written.

MAKE this comment:

- This completes our module on planning. When we return from our break, we'll begin the module on organizing. Right now, we'll take a 15-minute break.

00:15   **Break**

Notes   •   _____

•   _____

•   _____

•   _____

•   _____

•   _____

•   _____

•   _____

•   _____

•   _____

•   _____

•   _____

3. Organizing Tasks and People (25 min.)

Purpose

The purpose of this module is to identify what organizing tasks participants perform, and to create an action plan to achieve the appropriate balance between organizing and other supervisory functions.

Objectives

As a result of this module, participants will be able to:

- Identify organizing tasks that they perform.

- Assess whether they spend the right amount of time on organizing tasks.

- Create an action plan to achieve the appropriate balance between organizing and other supervisory functions.

- Use eight key organizing questions as analytical tools.

Workshop Agenda

3. Organizing Tasks and People	Minutes 25	Start/Stop 10:05 / 10:30	Actual Start / Stop
Module Overview	5	10:05 / 10:10	_____ / _____
Organizing Survey	15	10:10 / 10:25	_____ / _____
Key Organizing Questions	4	10:25 / 10:29	_____ / _____
Module Summary	1	10:29 / 10:30	_____ / _____

FACILITATOR COMMENTARY

00:05   **Module Overview**

 DISTRIBUTE the handout, *Key Organizing Questions* (p. 129) and the assessment, *Organizing Survey* (pp. 196-197).

MAKE these comments:

- This workshop module covers organizing tasks and people. During the next twenty-five minutes, we'll do the following:

    – Complete an *Organizing Survey* that is similar to the *Planning Survey*.

    – Learn eight key organizing questions you can use as analytical tools.

- In the supervision process, the organizing function follows the planning function. When supervisors organize tasks and people, they sequence the steps needed to reach the goal in a deliberate, purposeful manner. After listing the tasks involved, supervisors develop a schedule and decide what resources are required. Next, supervisors divide the work and delegate it. Then, like an orchestra conductor, the supervisor coordinates employee efforts so people work harmoniously toward a common goal.

00:15   **Organizing Survey**

 REFER participants to the *Organizing Survey* (pp. 196-197).

INDIVIDUAL ACTIVITY

 MAKE these comments:

- Refer to your *Organizing Survey*, which is similar to the Planning Survey that you completed earlier. Like the Planning Survey, the *Organizing Survey* gives you the opportunity to identify organizing tasks that you perform, assess whether you spend the right amount of time on these tasks, and list actions you will take when you return to the workplace to arrive at the appropriate balance between organizing and other supervisory functions.

- You have ten minutes to complete the survey and action plan. Begin now.

 CALL time when ten minutes have elapsed.

GROUP DISCUSSION

ASK these questions:

- What activities listed on the survey take up too much of your time, and what actions will you take?

- What activities listed on the survey require more time, and what actions will you take?

FACILITATOR COMMENTARY

SUMMARIZE the discussion to conclude the activity.

00:04   **Key Organizing Questions**

REFER participants to the handout, *Key Organizing Questions*, (p. 129).

MAKE this comment:

- When organizing work, supervisors should consider the questions on the handout, *Key Organizing Questions* (p. 129). Please take the next two minutes to read that handout.

ASK for and *ANSWER* any questions.

00:01   **Module Summary**

MAKE these summary points about organizing:

- Organizing follows planning in the supervision process.

- When supervisors organize work, they are like orchestra conductors, coordinating employee efforts so people work harmoniously toward a common goal.

Notes

- _____

- _____

- _____

- _____

- _____

- _____

- _____

- _____

4. Delegating (1 hr. 15 min.)

Purpose	The purpose of this module is to describe the delegation process, allow participants to plan the delegation of an assignment, and to provide skill practice.
Objectives	As a result of this module, participants will be able to:

- Describe a six-step delegation process.

- Plan how to delegate an assignment when they return to work.

- Practice delegating an assignment.

- Receive feedback on their delegation skill-practice.

Workshop Agenda

4. Delegating	Minutes 1 hr. 15	Start/Stop 10:30 / 11:45	Actual Start / Stop
Module Overview	5	10:30 / 10:35	_____ / _____
Benefits of Delegating	5	10:35 / 10:40	_____ / _____
Barriers to Delegating	5	10:40 / 10:45	_____ / _____
Delegation Process	12	10:45 / 10:57	_____ / _____
Delegation Planning	8	10:57 / 11:05	_____ / _____
Delegation Skill-Practice	25	11:05 / 11:30	_____ / _____
Module Summary	1	11:30 / 11:31	_____ / _____
Workshop Summary	4	11:31 / 11:35	_____ / _____
Workshop Evaluations	10	11:35 / 11:45	_____ / _____
Total (including one fifteen-minute break)	**3.75 hours**		

FACILITATOR COMMENTARY

00:05   **Module Overview**

 MAKE this comment:

- Since delegation is a key component of the organizing function, we'll take an in-depth look at that topic.

FACILITATOR COMMENTARY

 REVIEW the module objectives.

 DISTRIBUTE the participant handout, *What Is Delegation?* (p. 130).

 MAKE this comment:

- Delegation is the assignment of responsibilities and obligations to others, along with authority and resources necessary to complete the job. When supervisors delegate, they accomplish results for which they are accountable by empowering others.

00:05   **Benefits of Delegating**

GROUP DISCUSSION

 ASK the following question:

- What are the benefits of delegating?

 WRITE answers on a chart pad.

LOOK for answers that make the following points:

- Increases the supervisor's productivity.
- Strengthens the work team. Builds backup capabilities for peak load times, vacations, or emergencies.
- Provides variety in assignments, which can increase job satisfaction and fight boredom.
- Allows employees to show their capabilities.
- Motivates and rewards employees with challenging assignments.
- Gives employees a chance to grow professionally.
- Builds employee pride and self-esteem.
- Can lead to better decisions.
- Can produce results faster.

POST the chart paper on the wall.

00:05 **Barriers to Delegating**

 ASK the following question:

- What are the barriers to delegating?

 WRITE answers on a chart pad.

LOOK for answers that make the points that follow. Note: The accompanying parenthetical notes provide the facilitator with possible responses to participants' objections to delegating.

- It's faster for the supervisor to do the job than to teach an employee. (Training employees to do recurring jobs saves the supervisor time in the long run.)

- Reluctance to give up preferred activities. (Supervisors are supposed to accomplish work through others.)

- Delegation isn't feasible because the deadline is too close. (This predicament suggests management isn't planning and organizing effectively and/or that employees need skill training.)

- Lack of confidence in others. (To discover and build employee skills, the supervisor should delegate more, not less.)

- Fear of losing control. (Establishing and monitoring controls is an essential step in the delegation process.)

- Threat of competition from an exceptionally good worker. (When a member of the work team shines, the light reflects positively on the supervisor and the work unit. The supervisor's chances of promotion are better when he is not seen as indispensable.)

- Fear of being resented by employees. (Delegation can build employee motivation and confidence. Failure to delegate can cause resentment and undermine employee self-confidence. Supervisors can create resentment when they habitually dump undesirable tasks on employees or distribute the work load unfairly.)

 POST the chart paper on the wall.

FACILITATOR COMMENTARY

00:12   **Delegation Process**

SHOW and *DISTRIBUTE* the overhead transparency, *Delegation Process* (p. 221).

MAKE these comments:

- Delegation is a six-step process that includes planning the work, organizing it, presenting the project to the employee, involving the employee, empowering the employee, and tracking progress and providing support. Let's examine each step.

  1. Plan the work.

  The delegation process begins when you analyze tasks to be accomplished and plan how they are to be performed.

  2. Organize the work.

  Divide responsibilities among employees and decide how much authority to transfer. When mapping out assignments, consider employees' capabilities, experience, interests, and current work priorities. At times, you must adjust the workload to free an employee for a new assignment.

  3. Present the project.

  When making the assignment, cover the following:

  – Background on the assignment.

  – Why the employee was selected to do the job.

  – Advantages for the employee.

  – What outcome is desired.

  – What to do and how to do it. (The amount of detail depends on the employee's experience level. A recently hired worker may need step-by-step instructions. With experienced employees, it's generally better to describe end results, not methods of achieving the results.)

  – When and where to perform the work.

  – Due date, along with any intermediate milestones.

  – Extent of authority being delegated.

  – Budget and other resources available.

  – How performance will be measured.

4. Involve the employee.

Delegation is a two-way street. You must pass responsibility and commensurate authority to the employee. The employee, in turn, must be willing to accept the delegation. Consequently, effective delegators involve employees in defining the scope of work, describing results, setting the schedule, and establishing controls. Typical controls are quality, quantity, cost, and due dates. To avoid misunderstandings, ask employees to describe the assignment. Finally, invite questions and offer support.

GROUP DISCUSSION

 ASK this question:

• What should a supervisor do when an employee doesn't want to accept an assignment?

LOOK for answers that make the following points:

• The supervisor needs to find out why the employee objects.

• If workers lack confidence, the supervisor can give specific examples of successful past performance which show that they can do the job.

• If the worker has a legitimate concern, the supervisor may want to modify the assignment or give the job to someone else.

• If the worker remains uncooperative, the supervisor should consult with his or her manager and human resources to evaluate alternatives, including discipline.

 RESUME the commentary.

5. Empower the employee.

Once you delegate an assignment, you must enable the employee by providing the time and resources to do the job. You must also empower the employee by publicizing the assignment and asking others to cooperate. Then it's time to back away and let the responsible employee do the job.

 ASK this question:

• If people bypass the individual a supervisor has delegated work to by bringing matters directly to the supervisor, what should the supervisor do?

LOOK for answers that make the following point:

• The supervisor should uphold the delegation by saying something like, "Please see Tom about that. I've delegated the responsibility to him."

RESUME the commentary.

6. Track progress and provide support.

At agreed-upon intervals, review progress via meetings, reading reports, or practicing "Management by Walking Around." When the responsible employees seek help or need redirection, answer questions, provide coaching, or find resources. Hold employees responsible for completing their assignments. Finally, reward good performance.

FACILITATOR COMMENTARY

00:08   **Delegation Planning**

 MAKE the following comment:

- The next activity will give you an opportunity to plan the delegation of an assignment that you want performed, as well as to practice actually delegating the assignment to the employee.

INDIVIDUAL ACTIVITY

 DISTRIBUTE the learning activity, *Delegation Planning Worksheet* (p. 168).

 MAKE the following comment:

- Think of a task that you will delegate when you return to work. If you cannot think of a work-related assignment, use a task you want performed at home. You can also use a task you have delegated in the past. Completing the *Delegation Planning Worksheet* will help you to think through critical elements of the task. It will also help you to identify employees who can do the job. You have five minutes to complete the worksheet.

 CALL time when five minutes have elapsed.

FACILITATOR COMMENTARY

00:25   **Delegation Skill-Practice**

 DISTRIBUTE three copies of the learning activity, *Delegation Skill-Practice: Observer Checklist* (p. 169).

 MAKE this comment:

- It is as important for supervisors to practice their skills in a classroom learning laboratory as it is for an athlete to practice on the playing field. For that reason, the next activity is a skill practice. The delegation planning exercise that you just completed will be the basis of the skill practice.

 SHOW the overhead transparency, *Round-Robin Skill-Practice* (p. 223).

- There will be three skill-practice rounds so that each person can practice delegating an assignment to an employee, who will be played by another member of the trio. The third person serves as the observer and timekeeper. At the conclusion of each round, the observer gives feedback using the *Delegation Skill-Practice: Observer Checklist*. The "supervisor" and "employee" also give their reactions.

- This overhead transparency illustrates how each member of the trio plays a different part in each round of the skill practice. If there are four in a group, the fourth person serves as an observer, also.

- You'll have five minutes for each round of practice and feedback.

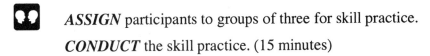
GROUP ACTIVITY

 ASSIGN participants to groups of three for skill practice.

CONDUCT the skill practice. (15 minutes)

 CALL time at five minute intervals.

GROUP DISCUSSION

 ASK for volunteers to share what they learned.

FACILITATOR COMMENTARY

00:01   **Module Summary**

MAKE these summary points about delegating:

- Delegation is the assignment of responsibilities and obligations to others, along with authority and resources necessary to complete the job.

- When supervisors delegate, they accomplish results for which they are accountable by empowering others.

- Delegation increases the supervisor's productivity and strengthens the work team.

00:04　　　　　　　**Workshop Summary**

MAKE these comments:

- Today we have accomplished the following:

  - Completed a *Planning Survey.*

  - Created an action plan to achieve the appropriate balance between planning and other supervisory functions.

  - Described a seven-step method for developing and implementing plans.

  - Completed an *Organizing Survey.*

  - Created an action plan to achieve the appropriate balance between organizing and other supervisory functions.

  - Described a six-step delegation process.

  - Planned how to delegate an assignment when you return to work.

  - Practiced delegating the assignment.

  - Received feedback on your skill practice.

- You've been an outstanding group. Thank you for your participation. Good luck.

00:10　　　　　　　**Evaluations**

MAKE this comment:

- We'd appreciate some feedback from each of you about the workshop. I'm going to distribute an evaluation form. Please complete it now. Afterward, place the form on the table by the door, and you are free to leave. Again, thank you and good luck.

DISTRIBUTE the *Program Evaluation* (p. 212).

Notes

- _____

- _____

- _____

- _____

- _____

- _____

Chapter Six

One-Hour Supervision Workshop

This chapter contains the training plan for your one-hour supervision workshop—ready to go "as is" or to be tailored to meet your needs. The chapter is divided into three parts:

- Workshop Agenda.

- Getting Ready.

- Training Plan.

"GIVING INSTRUCTIONS"

This workshop is designed for new or experienced supervisors. The purpose is to provide techniques for giving instructions, as well as skill practice and opportunities for observation. When participants have completed the session they will be able to:

- Avoid behaviors that inhibit the learning process.

- Use behaviors that encourage the learning process.

- Describe six communications techniques for giving clear instructions.

Workshop Agenda

Giving Instructions	Minutes 60	Start/Stop 8:00 / 9:00	Actual Start / Stop
Welcome	5	8:00 / 8:05	_____ / _____
Workshop Overview	5	8:05 / 8:10	_____ / _____
Preparation for Demonstration	8	8:10 / 8:18	_____ / _____
Reading—Giving Instructions: Extra Mile Athletic Shoes	5	8:18 / 8:23	_____ / _____
Demonstration—Giving Instructions: Extra Mile Athletic Shoes	8	8:23 / 8:31	_____ / _____
Question and Answer	13	8:31 / 8:44	_____ / _____
Tips for Giving Instructions	12	8:44 / 8:56	_____ / _____
Workshop Summary	4	8:56 / 9:00	_____ / _____

Getting Ready

Materials Needed

These are the materials recommended for the one-hour Giving Instructions workshop. Page references indicate where masters for the materials are found elsewhere in this book. Unless otherwise noted:

- For overhead transparencies, you will need one transparency each.

- For other items, you will need one per participant, plus a few spares.

Overhead Transparencies

☐ Giving Instructions (p. 222).

Handouts

☐ Giving Instructions (p. 222).

Learning Activities

☐ Giving Instructions (pp. 170-174).

- One Supervisor's background sheet (p. 171).

- One Employee's background sheet (p. 172).

- Observers' background sheet for all participants except those playing the "supervisor" and "employee," (p. 173).

- Giving Instructions Skill-Practice: Observer Checklist for all participants except those playing the "supervisor" and "employee" (p. 174).

- One large, colorful new tennis shoe with lace removed.

- One shoe lace.

Tailoring Tips

To tailor the workshop to your particular group, do the following:

- For ease in distributing and referring to materials in class, create a numbered handout packet. Bind or staple the packet.

- Design a custom cover similar to the example below with the name of the sponsoring organization, date, and place of the workshop, and print it on heavy paper (cover stock).

- Distribute the packet when you begin the workshop and refer participants to appropriate pages throughout the workshop.

Sample Custom Cover

Giving Instructions

Sponsored by
Straight Laced Services

Date
Location

Things to Do

Prior to conducting the workshop, do the following:

☑ **Prepare materials.**

Before you present the workshop, photocopy the workshop agenda and script. Write your planned start/stop times and anecdotal material on the photocopy.

☑ **Inquire about special needs.**

Meet with the director of training and several of the individuals enrolled in the course to learn about any special needs, internal issues, and the experience level of participants.

☑ **Develop relevant examples.**

Develop examples that are relevant to the industry or enterprise.

☑ **Encourage management participation.**

Invite a middle or top manager to kick off the workshop and emphasize the important role played by supervisors.

Training Plan

Giving Instructions (1 hr.)

FACILITATOR COMMENTARY

00:05

Welcome

WELCOME participants to this workshop on giving instructions.

INTRODUCE yourself and give a brief summary of your qualifications and background.

TELL participants to write their names on the name cards at their places.

REVIEW the following housekeeping details:

- Workshop length.

- Smoking policy.

- Location of rest rooms, telephones, and fire exits.

00:05

Workshop Overview

INTRODUCE the workshop.

- Supervisors spend a large percentage of their work day giving instructions. Sometimes the result is exactly what you wanted. Other times, you are left shaking your head in dismay, asking, "Why in the world did the employee do *THAT*?"

- Do things go well because the supervisor gives clear instructions or because the employee is good at figuring out what the supervisor *intended* rather than what the supervisor *said*?

- Do things go wrong because the employee doesn't listen, or because the supervisor leaves out important details?

- Sometimes the more you know about a task, the more difficult it is to tell another person how to perform it. That's often because the process of completing the task has become so integrated in your mind that you forget to mention essential steps. For instance, driving a car can become so automatic that many an unhappy parent has neglected to tell a teenage protege, "Be sure the car is in reverse gear before you try to drive out of the garage!" On the other hand, you don't want to be so explicit that you appear patronizing or rule out all creativity or initiative.

- Even when you methodically list every step in a process, there can be breakdowns in interpersonal communication. For example, common words can have very different meanings for each party to a transaction, resulting in misunderstandings.

- As a result of our next activity, *Giving Instructions*, you will:

    - Practice communicating instructions.

    - Observe others communicating instructions.

    - Practice following instructions.

    - Observe others following instructions.

    - Be able to describe six communications techniques for giving clear instructions.

GROUP ACTIVITY

00:08   **Preparation for Demonstration**

 ASK for two volunteers.

 GIVE volunteer number one the following materials:

- Copy of the supervisor's background sheet from the learning activity, *Giving Instructions* (p. 171).

- Tennis shoe.

- Shoe lace.

 MAKE this comment to volunteer number one:

- In this activity, you will practice the part of a supervisor giving instructions to a new employee. Your job is to teach volunteer number two, the employee, to lace and tie the tennis shoe. Here is a copy of the supervisor's background sheet. Please leave the room for five minutes and read the background material. Plan how you will give instructions to the employee during the skill practice. I'll call you back into the classroom when it is time to begin the activity.

MAKE these comments to volunteer number two after volunteer number one leaves the room:

- During this demonstration, you will practice the part of a new employee at Straight Laced Services. Your job is to lace and tie shoes that will be sold by Extra Mile Athletic Shoes, a retail chain. Since you have no prior experience lacing or tying shoes, your supervisor will teach you to do the task. As the employee, your role is to act naive, take each instruction literally, and do only what you are told. Forget that you have ever laced or tied a shoe before. Please read this background sheet.

GIVE volunteer number two the employee background sheet from the Learning Activity, *Giving Instructions* (p. 172).

DISTRIBUTE the observer background sheet from the Learning Activity, *Giving Instructions* (p. 173), to the rest of the class and ask them to read the material.

INDIVIDUAL ACTIVITY

00:05

Reading—Giving Instructions: Extra Mile Athletic Shoes

MAKE these comments:

- You have just received copies of the observer background sheets from the learning activity, *Giving Instructions* . So that you will be better prepared to watch and learn from the demonstration that we are about to have, please read the background sheets. Pay special attention to the observer checklist on the third page. Keep the checklist in mind as you watch the skill practice. Be prepared to comment on your observations following the skill practice.

SEND one of the participants to bring volunteer number one back to the classroom.

00:08

Demonstration—Giving Instructions: Extra Mile Athletic Shoes

POSITION both volunteers where they can be seen by all.

CONDUCT the demonstration.

CALL time on the demonstration.

GROUP DISCUSSION

00:13   **Question and Answer**

 ASK the "employee" the following questions:

- What difficulties did you have following the directions you were given? Why?

- What did the supervisor do that helped you learn the task?

- What could the supervisor have done to help you master the task more quickly or easily?

- What could you have done to help the supervisor teach you the task?

 ASK the "supervisor" the following questions:

- What difficulties did you have giving directions? Why?

- What techniques worked best?

- What could you have done differently?

 THANK the two volunteers for their participation, and *LEAD* a round of applause.

 ASK these questions from the *Giving Instructions Skill-Practice: Observer Checklist* and look for answers that make the following points:

1. **What communications techniques did the supervisor use that helped the employee learn the task?**

   - Gave background on the assignment.

   - Explained importance of the assignment.

   - Described end result.

   - Explained each step in the process in clear, simple language.

   - Used relevant examples.

   - Demonstrated each step in the process before asking the employee to perform the step.

   - Praised the employee for correct behavior.

   - Encouraged the employee.

2. **What behaviors did the supervisor use that made it more difficult for the employee to learn the task?**

   - Used complicated language.

   - Made the task sound or look difficult.

   - Displayed a lack of interest or confidence in the employee.

   - Left out steps in the process.

   - Asked, "Do you understand?" or "Have I made myself clear?"

   - Showed impatience or frustration.

   - Neglected to have the employee explain and demonstrate the process.

3. **What did the employee do to help the learning process?**

   - Was cooperative.

   - Showed a willing attitude.

   - Listened and watched carefully.

   - Asked questions.

   - Practiced the necessary behaviors.

   - Was optimistic about his or her ability to master the task.

   - Was careful to meet performance standards.

   - Was adaptable.

   - Was creative.

4. **What did the employee do that inhibited the learning process?**

   - Appeared disinterested.

   - Was overconfident.

   - Didn't accept direction well.

   - Resented being asked to practice.

   - Didn't listen and watch.

   - Didn't ask questions.

   - Was too creative.

FACILITATOR COMMENTARY

00:12

Tips for Giving Instructions

SHOW and *DISTRIBUTE* the overhead transparency, *Giving Instructions* (p. 222).

MAKE the following comment:

- Here are six techniques to use when giving instructions:

1. **List each step.**

   List every step required to complete the task. Ask yourself, "What mini-steps or special techniques does a novice need to be told about?" Ask a knowledgeable coworker to review your list for completeness.

2. **Show and tell.**

   Show the employee how to do the task as you are telling. Show examples of finished work.

3. **Watch body language.**

   Pay attention to body language. Does the employee look puzzled, confused, or worried?

4. **Check for understanding.**

   Ask employees to tell you what they are going to do and to show you how they will do it.

GROUP DISCUSSION

ASK this question and look for answers that make the following points:

- Why is it a poor practice to ask, "Do you understand?" or "Have I made myself clear?"

  - To avoid appearing stupid and to save face, most employees usually say yes even when they don't understand.

  - The questions sound parental and convey the message that the relationship between the supervisor and employee is a parent-child one, rather than adult to adult.

FACILITATOR COMMENTARY

 RESUME your facilitator commentary.

5. Clarify misconceptions.

- Clarify any misconceptions the employee may have. Use different examples and different language.

- Demonstrate the process again. Continue clarifying and redirecting the employee until the employee understands and can perform the task.

- Keep in mind that being able to explain how to do a task does not necessarily mean the person can actually perform the task. For example, someone may be able to explain how to change a tire, but not have the physical strength or mechanical aptitude to use the jack, undo lug nuts, or remove and replace the tire.

6. Check on progress.

Check on progress frequently until the employee exhibits full mastery. Then check occasionally to let the employee know you care and appreciate the good work. If the employee has fallen into poor habits, redirect behavior.

 ASK for and *ANSWER* any questions.

00:04

Workshop Summary

 MAKE these comments:

- Productivity depends on your ability to communicate instructions clearly and completely to employees.

- In the *Giving Instructions: Extra Mile Athletic Shoe* demonstration, you saw how techniques such as showing and telling and asking for feedback helped the communication process.

- Keep the six tips for giving instructions handy, and refer to it before giving an employee an assignment.

- Thank you for your participation. You've been a great group. Good luck in your careers as supervisors.

Chapter Seven:

Participant Handouts

In this chapter, you will find masters from which you can create participant handouts for use during your supervision training sessions.

USING HANDOUT MASTERS

You may use the handout masters in two ways:

- Key them into your word processing system "as is" or customize them to suit your specific needs.

- Photocopy the masters that you need from this book and use them "as is."

The Basics of Supervision

What Is Supervision?

Supervisors occupy the first rung on the management ladder. They focus the efforts of operating (nonmanagerial) employees to accomplish the enterprise's goals. In control-oriented, hierarchical organizations, supervision is direct, day-to-day, hour-by-hour, hands-on management. In more participative, networked environments, supervisors may play a more diffused role as ad hoc team leaders, facilitators, or coaches.

What Is Management?

Management is a four-step process of planning, organizing, leading, and controlling an enterprise's resources to achieve its mission and objectives. These four steps are interdependent functions in a dynamic cycle that can be interrupted at any point. For example, during the planning phase of a project, controls such as target dates are established. For any number of reasons, some outside the team's control, the schedule can slip, making revisions to the plan and target dates necessary.

Managers at every level perform the four-step process of planning, organizing, leading, and controlling to achieve the enterprise's mission and objectives. What differs at each level is the focus managers take as they perform their functions. Top management takes a long-term strategic focus, middle management an intermediate focus, and first-line supervisors a near-term operational focus.

The principles of management apply to any organization: for-profit and not-for-profit, public sector and private, small and large, manufacturing and service.

Management Levels

Most organizations have three broad management levels: executive or top management, middle management, and first-line supervision. In large organizations, each level can have several sublevels within it.

In addition, there generally are two streams—line and staff. *Line* managers oversee line functions, which are activities central to producing the enterprise's products and services; for instance, engineering, production, manufacturing, finance, marketing, and sales. *Staff* managers direct units that support the line organization by performing analyses, advising, or providing internal services; for instance, human resources, legal, public relations, administrative services, information systems, or materials management.

Top Managers/Executives

Taking a long-term focus, the top management team provides overall direction for the entire enterprise. Its members develop the enterprise's vision, mission, strategic plan, goals, and policies. They are the architects who design the enterprise's structure. Top management is concerned with external forces such as general economic conditions, the political climate, legislation, and public opinion.

Mid-Level Managers

Mid-level managers occupy the tier in the organizational pyramid that falls between the executive level and the supervisory level. The upper layer of middle managers reports directly to top management. The trend is to reduce the number of middle managers. Middle managers plan and implement programs that carry out objectives and directives set by top management. Also, they direct the work of supervisors and some staff specialists.

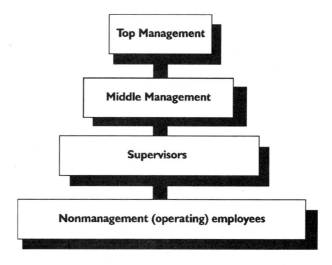

Supervisors

Supervisors direct the daily efforts of nonmanagerial employees who do the hands-on work. In addition to performing the management functions of planning, organizing, leading, and controlling, supervisors have the following seven basic responsibilities which are described by Bradford Boyd in his classic text for supervisors, *Management-Minded Supervision* (Second edition, New York: McGraw-Hill Book Company, 1976).

1. **Production.**

   Delivering the product or service with the available resources.

2. **Morale.**

   Stimulating a positive work attitude on the part of employees.

3. **Quality.**

   Stimulating quality-consciousness and job pride in the workforce.

4. **Costs.**

   Contributing to the enterprise's profitability by cost control and cost reduction.

5. **Methods.**

   Seeking easier and better ways of doing work.

6. **Training.**

   Teaching employees how to perform their jobs and stay current with changing technology.

7. **Safety.**

   Minimizing risks and hazards in the work area.

According to Boyd, each of these responsibilities requires supervisory attention. Their relative importance may change from time to time, but none can be overlooked for very long.

Supervisory Roles

Each day supervisors assume a variety of roles as they interact with other people. A role is a character that the supervisor assumes in a particular situation, much like an actor plays a role in a film. Here are some typical roles:

Coach

Develops game plans and calls plays; makes assignments; encourages team members; assesses strengths and developmental needs; builds individual and team strengths by training; allows members to practice skills; gives feedback.

Team captain

Uses leadership and communication skills to build teams and hold them together; inspires confidence; communicates the vision, mission, and goals of the enterprise to team members; guides teams in development of objectives; helps members understand the positions they play; seeks participation in team projects; openly confronts conflicts.

Cheerleader

Encourages team members to excel; shows and builds confidence in abilities of team members; generates enthusiasm and support for team projects both within the immediate group and from the organization as a whole.

News reporter

Communicates information within the team; promotes the team to others.

Fortune teller

Projects trends; decides or recommends best course of action based on these predictions.

Political analyst

Analyzes the current politics of the enterprise and develops strategies accordingly.

Counselor

Listens to employee problems; helps employees develop solutions.

Parent

Supports and nurtures employees.

Referee

Calls time out during conflicts; seeks resolution; determines penalties.

Negotiator

Is an honest broker in bringing people with different views together; negotiates for resources.

Gladiator

Battles to gain support or resources; fights to protect the team or project.

Hunter

Openly seeks new projects and sources of work for the team.

Resource allocator

Determines or recommends how the team's resources will be used.

Spokesperson

Represents the organization at professional, civic, or other meetings.

Detective

Jointly identifies problems, determines causes, and develops solutions.

Creating Goals and Objectives

Creating goals and objectives for a plan begins with selecting key result areas (KRA). KRAs are subject areas where high performance is essential to fulfillment of the unit's mission. Potential KRAs include productivity, quality, customer service, innovation, process and methods improvement, training, safety, scrap reduction, time conservation, cost reduction, housekeeping, and environmental responsibility.

Next, identify goals for each key result area. Goals are end results. Goal statements describe what results the unit wants to achieve within a time period, say one year. It takes a series of actions to reach a goal. Statements describing these actions are termed "objectives." Well-crafted objectives meet the following criteria:

- **Specific.**

  Objectives must be written in clear language that describes what will be done and by whom.

- **Time-limited.**

  Objectives must include a completion date, and intermediate milestones.

- **Realistic.**

  Resources such as staff, equipment, space, and funds must be available or obtainable. Time estimates must be realistic. To estimate time, take an optimistic, pessimistic, and most likely estimate, and then apply the following formula:

$$\frac{\text{Optimistic} + \text{Pessimistic} + 4(\text{Most Likely})}{6} = \text{Estimated Time}$$

- **Measurable.**

  Objectives should contain a standard of performance by which success can be measured. Standards might be time, quantity, cost, or quality. Whenever possible, use numerical standards.

Key Organizing Questions

When organizing work, supervisors should consider the following:

- **Why is the project being done?**

- **How else might the end result be attained?**

- **Where is the project being done?**

- **Could the project be accomplished more efficiently elsewhere?**

- **When is the project being done?**

- **Is there a better time to work on the project?**

- **Who are the best people to work on the project?**

- **What technologies can we employ to increase productivity, raise quality, or otherwise add value?**

What Is Delegation?

Delegation is the assignment of responsibilities and obligations to others, along with authority and resources necessary to complete the job. When supervisors delegate, they accomplish results for which they are accountable by empowering others.

Authority gives a supervisor the right to make decisions, carry out actions, and direct others. When a supervisor delegates authority, the degree of authority granted can range from complete to none.

- Complete authority allows the employee to decide and act without consulting a superior.

- Limited authority allows the employee to:

  - decide, act without consulting a superior, and then report routinely, or

  - decide, act, and tell the superior immediately.

- Employees with no authority must:

  - recommend action, obtain superior's approval, and act,

  - seek superior's advice and then take action, or

  - act only after instructed by the superior.

It's unrealistic and unfair to assign responsibility to employees without giving them sufficient authority to accomplish their mission. Authority and responsibility must coincide.

Supervisors can delegate authority and responsibility, but they are still accountable to upper management and to the enterprise for both the successes and mistakes made by employees.

Leading

Leading is the process of influencing other people to follow in the achievement of a common goal.

To lead effectively, supervisors must make positive use of power. Power is the ability to influence the behavior of others.

There are two kinds of power: position power and personal power. Position power is derived from the formal authority that the enterprise vests in the supervisor. Personal power is based on personal characteristics or inspirational qualities that make others want to follow a particular individual.

Components of position power include the power to reward or coerce employees, as well as the power to share or withhold information. Rewards can come in the form of preferred assignments, work schedules, and vacation times; pay increases; awards, and training. The supervisor's power to coerce rests in the authority to discipline, give unsatisfactory performance reviews, and withhold desired rewards.

While the enterprise vests position power in the supervisor, the employee-followers grant personal power to the supervisor-leader. The granting of personal power occurs because the followers respect or like the leader, or because they see their goals being satisfied by the goals of the leader.

Characteristics that enhance personal power include a clear vision, sense of mission, energy, moral force, strength of character, the ability to motivate and communicate, persuasiveness, self-confidence, courage, extraversion, competence, integrity, honesty, and charisma.

Leadership and Motivation

Motivation is the stimulus that causes a person to act. Most psychologists agree that supervisors can't actually motivate employees to perform their jobs. The spark or motivation must come from within the employee. Supervisors can use their leadership skills to enroll employee-followers in a vision and offer rewards for turning vision into reality.

External forces also can cause us to act; but, as soon as the force diminishes, so does motivation. For instance, supervisors might obtain short-term results by threatening employees, but these techniques don't create long-term motivation. They often lead to employee resentment and resistance.

When supervisors foster self-motivation in employees, they are leading and inspiring employees to apply energy to achieve organizational goals. In addition to using their leadership skills to enhance motivation, supervisors can also influence motivation during the planning, organizing, and controlling stages of the management process.

By involving employees in planning, organizing the work, and defining how performance will be measured (controlling), supervisors can build commitment to a shared vision. That commitment can become the internal spark that ignites personal motivation. It's equally motivating when supervisors give employees frequent feedback, including offering praise, making suggestions for improvement, and expressing appreciation for employee efforts.

Controlling

Controlling involves setting standards, measuring performance against those standards, rewarding desired behaviors and taking corrective action when necessary.

The most common controls are:

- **Time.**

  Completion schedules, shipment and delivery dates.

- **Quantity.**

  Volume of work an employee accomplishes; number of pieces produced.

- **Quality.**

  Extent to which work, products, or services meet standards, specifications, or customer expectations. Measures include percentage of rejects, amount of scrap, number of complaints, and customer approval ratings.

- **Cost.**

  Amount of money spent to produce goods and services, usually in relation to a budget.

- **Material.**

  Limits on inventory of raw materials, work-in-progress materials, and finished goods kept on hand. Usually stated in pounds, pieces, or gallons.

- **Behavioral.**

  Focuses on the human element by setting standards of behavior for workers.

The Control Process

There are four steps in the control process: setting standards, measuring performance, comparing results with standards, and taking action.

1. **Set performance standards.**

   Standards describe expectations and allowable deviations as specifically as possible. The extent of deviation, or tolerance, allowed depends on the precision required.

2. **Measure performance.**

   The nature of the work and the performance standards usually determine how often supervisors measure performance. For many activities, supervisors may want to measure weekly, daily, hourly, or even more frequently.

3. **Compare performance with standards.**

   Analyze the information gathered and look for gaps between standards and actual performance.

4. **Take necessary action.**

   When standards are met or exceeded, it's essential to reinforce desired behavior by rewarding performance. Recognition methods include verbal praise, letters of commendation, honorary or monetary awards, bonuses, salary increases, training, and special assignments.

   When standards are not being met, supervisors must identify and correct the problem, and prevent it from happening again.

   When conditions change, standards and measures may need to be adjusted accordingly. For example, if a work team consistently exceeds its production quotas, the control standard could be adjusted upward. In a case where a quota appears unrealistically high, it should be revised downward.

Chapter Eight:

Learning Activities

This chapter contains learning activities for use during your supervision training sessions.

USING THE LEARNING ACTIVITIES

Before each learning activity, you'll find instructions on its use. In cases where the facilitator needs sample answers, an annotated facilitator's copy of the learning activity precedes the participants' version. You may use the activities in two ways:

- Key them into your word processing system "as is" or customize them to suit your specific needs.

- Photocopy the learning activities that you need from this book and use them "as is."

Get-Acquainted Treasure Hunt

Description

This learning activity can be used with groups of between twenty and thirty participants as an icebreaker at the beginning of a workshop, as an energizer anytime, or as a closing activity. As a closing activity, the treasure hunt serves as a content review, and it lets participants obtain names of people they want to add to their network.

Objectives

As a result of this activity, participants will be able to:

*   Build a support network with other participants.

*   Discuss different points of view about supervision.

The trainer will be able to:

*   Assess the experience level and management philosophy of participants.

Time

*   30 minutes.

Materials

*   A copy of *Get Acquainted Treasure Hunt* (p. 137) for each participant.

*   Prizes for the first five people to obtain fifteen signatures.

Procedure

1. Tell participants that building a network is an important by-product of workshops. Each person in your network is a treasure of information, help, and support. This learning activity provides an opportunity to expand your network.
    (1 minute)

2. Ask participants to obtain the signatures of fifteen people who fit one of the descriptions or who agree with one of the statements on the sheet you are about to distribute. A person can only sign each sheet once. Fifteen different signatures are needed to complete the exercise. Tell participants that when they obtain fifteen signatures, let the facilitator know immediately, because the first five people to finish will receive a prize. Participants will have ten minutes to obtain signatures. (2 minutes)

3. Distribute copies of the learning activity (p. 137). Give participants three minutes to read the handout, and begin the treasure hunt. (5 minutes)

4. When five people have obtained all fifteen signatures, or after ten minutes have passed, call time and ask participants to return to their seats. (10 minutes)

5. Present prizes to the winners. (2 minutes)

6. Read each of the twenty statements aloud and ask for a show of hands indicating who fits the description or agrees with the statement. (9 minutes)

7. Conclude with a summary. (1 minute)

<u>HANDOUT</u>	**Get-Acquainted Treasure Hunt**
Directions	Obtain the signatures of fifteen people who fit one of the descriptions or who agree with one of the statements that follow. A person can only sign your sheet once, so you must find fifteen people to sign your sheet. When you have fifteen different signatures, let the facilitator know.

Signatures   **Descriptions**

_____   1. Supervises ten or more people.

_____   2. Is a new supervisor (zero to six months as a supervisor).

_____   3. Hates paperwork.

_____   4. Agrees that supervisors should maintain tight control.

_____   5. Agrees that supervisors should be democratic and collaborative.

_____   6. Is a veteran supervisor (has been in supervision five or more years).

_____   7. Agrees that safety is the supervisor's number-one priority.

_____   8. Would rather be back at the office.

_____   9. Agrees that maintaining the quality of work is the supervisor's number-one priority.

_____   10. Agrees that planning is a waste of time.

_____   11. Agrees that planning is essential.

_____   12. Agrees that total quality management is just a fad.

_____   13. Thrives on change.

_____   14. Likes stability.

_____   15. Agrees that the work environment should be fun.

_____   16. Agrees that work is serious and the environment should be businesslike.

_____   17. Agrees that people are motivated primarily by challenging work.

_____   18. Agrees that people are motivated primarily by money.

_____   19. Enjoys paperwork.

_____   20. Supervises nine or fewer people.

TRAINER'S NOTES

He's Sinking Fast

Description

He's Sinking Fast is a discussion case that focuses on the challenges new supervisors face when they have had no supervisory training, lack political savvy, and have no support network. The case is suitable for audiences of new and potential supervisors, as well as experienced supervisors. Experienced supervisors should be encouraged to think of how they can help new supervisors in their career transitions.

Objectives

As a result of this activity, participants will be able to:

- Anticipate problems that operating employees encounter when they become supervisors.

- Develop strategies to make the transition from operating employee to supervisor.

Time

- 30 minutes.

Materials

- A copy of the case study, *He's Sinking Fast,* for each participant (p. 141).

Procedure

1. Using information in the One-Day Training Plan (pp. 75-79), give a short lecture on challenges new supervisors face as they make the transition from an operating employee to a management team member. (7 minutes)

2. Distribute the case study and give participants four minutes to read the case and answer the accompanying questions. (6 minutes)

3. Assign participants to teams of three or four people. Instruct the teams to discuss the case study and develop team answers to the questions. Let them know they will be expected to share their team responses with the entire class. Tell teams they have five minutes. (6 minutes)

4. Ask for volunteers to present team answers. Look for answers that make the points listed after each question on the facilitator's copy of the activity. (5 minutes)

5. Summarize and conclude the activity. (3 minutes)

Facilitator's Copy With Answers

Directions

Read the case study and answer the questions below. Be prepared to discuss your answers with your team, as well as with the entire class.

> Jim, a skilled machinist, was recently promoted to supervisor. Jim has a reputation for delivering quality, precision work on time. He was selected for the supervisory position because he has an outstanding track record as a machinist and his co-workers have high esteem for him.
>
> After a month on the job, Jim has come to you for advice. He has had no training in management or supervision, and he feels he is sinking fast under his new responsibilities. He's so new to management that he is naive about politics and procedures.

1. **How can Jim acquire the necessary skills in supervision before it's too late?**

   - Explain his predicament to his manager and request training.

   - Visit the organization's training department to learn what courses and other resources are available.

   - Read books, listen to audiotapes, or view videos on basic supervision.

   - Take a correspondence course.

   - Attend a college course or a seminar on the topic.

2. **How can Jim get smart about organizational politics and procedures?**

   - Seek help from his manager.

   - Find a knowledgeable lunch partner.

   - Ask his peers at the first-line supervisory level.

   - Find a coach in the organization.

   - Read the organization's policies and procedures manual and employee handbook.

   - Scan the bulletin boards for policy statements.

   - Ask a personnel specialist in the human resources department for a briefing.

Facilitator's Copy (cont.)

3. **What steps can Jim take to build a support system?**

    *   Seek out knowledgeable peers and potential mentors.

    *   Join employee organizations—for example, athletic teams, Toastmasters, clubs, special interest groups.

Notes

*   _____

*   _____

*   _____

*   _____

*   _____

*   _____

*   _____

*   _____

*   _____

*   _____

*   _____

*   _____

*   _____

*   _____

*   _____

*   _____

*   _____

*   _____

*   _____

*   _____

*   _____

*   _____

*   _____

HANDOUT

Directions

He's Sinking Fast

Read the case study and answer the questions below. Be prepared to discuss your answers with your team, as well as with the entire class.

> Jim, a skilled machinist, was recently promoted to supervisor. Jim has a reputation for delivering quality, precision work on time. He was selected for the supervisory position because he has an outstanding track record as a machinist and his co-workers have high esteem for him.
>
> After a month on the job, Jim has come to you for advice. He has had no training in management or supervision, and he feels he is sinking fast under his new responsibilities. He's so new to management that he is naive about politics and procedures.

1. **How can Jim acquire the necessary skills in supervision before it's too late?**

2. **How can Jim get smart about organizational politics and procedures?**

3. **What steps can Jim take to build a support system?**

Delivering Unpopular News

Description

This discussion case explores the conflicts that can result when supervisors must uphold management policies with which they disagree.

Objectives

As a result of this activity, participants will be able to:

- Anticipate problems new supervisors encounter as they make the transition from operating employee to supervisor.

- Develop strategies to make the transition from operating employee to supervisor.

- Develop solutions for typical problems supervisors experience as they accomplish work through others.

Time

- 30 minutes.

Materials

- A copy of the case study, *Delivering Unpopular News* (p. 145), for each participant.

Procedure

1. Using information in the One-Day Training Plan (pp. 75-79), give a short lecture on challenges new supervisors face as they make the transition from operating employee to a member of the management team. (7 minutes)

2. Distribute the case study and give participants four minutes to read the case and answer the accompanying questions. (6 minutes)

3. Assign participants to teams of three or four people. Instruct the teams to discuss the case study and develop team answers to the questions. Let them know they will be expected to share their team responses with the entire class. Tell teams they have five minutes. (6 minutes)

4. Ask for volunteers to present team answers. Look for answers that make the points listed after each question on the facilitator's copy of the activity. (5 minutes)

5. Summarize the discussion and conclude the activity. (3 minutes)

Facilitator's Copy With Answers

Directions

Read the case study and answer the questions below. Be prepared to discuss your answers with your team, as well as with the entire class.

> Judy recently has been promoted to a supervisory position. She has just come from a departmental staff meeting where she learned that the company has decided to take a "hard line" on personal phone calls made from office telephones. Effective immediately, employees must place all personal calls from a public pay telephone. Judy knows this will be unpopular news. In fact, she disagrees with the policy, believing that the time employees spend finding a phone and waiting in line will cost the employer more than a brief call made from the work station. She's also concerned about the effect the policy will have on Dan, a single parent, who keeps tabs on his two sons through brief after-school phone calls.

1. **What should Judy say as she informs her work unit of the new policy?**

   - Inform employees about the new policy.

   - Explain the company's reasons for the change.

   - Let employees express their concerns.

   - Acknowledge their concerns.

   - Promise to tell her manager about employee concerns.

   - Ask for employee cooperation.

2. **As a member of the management team, what are Judy's responsibilities to the employer?**

   - Judy should tell her manager why she disagrees with the policy.

   - Judy must support the policy in front of employees.

Facilitator's Copy (cont.)

3. **What are Judy's responsibilities to her employees?**

   • Meet with her employees as soon as possible so that they hear the news from Judy, not secondhand.

   • Provide the good business reasons for the policy.

   • Listen to employee views on the matter.

   • Let employees know when she has made their views known to management.

   • Enforce the policy fairly, but accommodate special circumstances when possible.

4. **How should Judy enforce the policy with Dan?**

   • Meet with Dan privately to discuss his situation.

   • Engage in creative problem solving.

   • Work out accommodations that are within Judy's authority, but in keeping with the spirit of the new policy.

   • Look for acceptable alternatives.

Notes

   • _____

   • _____

   • _____

   • _____

   • _____

   • _____

   • _____

   • _____

   • _____

   • _____

   • _____

   • _____

   • _____

   • _____

   • _____

   • _____

Delivering Unpopular News

Directions   Read the case study and answer the questions below. Be prepared
              to discuss your answers with your team, as well as with the entire
              class.

> Judy recently has been promoted to a supervisory position.
> She has just come from a departmental staff meeting where
> she learned that the company has decided to take a "hard line"
> on personal phone calls made from office telephones. Effective
> immediately, employees must place all personal calls from a
> public pay telephone. Judy knows this will be unpopular news.
> In fact, she disagrees with the policy, believing that the time
> employees spend finding a phone and waiting in line will cost
> the employer more than a brief call made from the work sta-
> tion. She's also concerned about the effect the policy will have
> on Dan, a single parent, who keeps tabs on his two sons
> through brief after-school phone calls.

1. **What should Judy say as she informs her work unit of the
    new policy?**

2. **As a member of the management team, what are Judy's
    responsibilities to the employer?**

3. **What are Judy's responsibilities to her employees?**

4. **How should Judy enforce the policy with Dan?**

Preserving the Friendship

Description

Preserving the Friendship is a case suitable for small group discussion. The case addresses the issues of role shift, preserving friendships formed prior to promotion, and responding to employee requests for preferential treatment.

Objectives

As a result of this activity, participants will be able to:

- Anticipate problems new supervisors encounter.

- Develop strategies to deal with the role shift that occurs when operating employees become supervisors.

- Develop strategies for dealing with employee requests for preferential treatment.

Time

- 30 to 60 minutes.

Materials

- A copy of the case study, *Preserving the Friendship* (p. 148), for each participant.

Procedure

1. Using information in the One-Day Training Plan (pp. 75-79), give a short lecture on challenges new supervisors face as they make the transition from operating employee to a member of the management team. Place special emphasis on role shift. (7 minutes)

2. Distribute the case study. Give participants four minutes to read the case and answer the accompanying questions. (6 minutes)

3. Assign participants to teams of three and give them five minutes to discuss the case and answer the questions. Tell teams to select a spokesperson to report on the discussion. (6 minutes)

4. Have teams give their reports. Look for answers that make the points listed after each question in the facilitator's copy of the activity. (5 minutes)

5. Summarize the discussion and conclude the activity. (3 minutes)

Facilitator's Copy With Answers

Directions

Read the case study and answer the questions below. Be prepared to discuss your answers with your team, as well as with the entire class.

> While a rank-and-file employee, Barry became good friends with Robert, an employee he now supervises. Barry now thinks Robert is trying to take advantage of their friendship by asking for preferential treatment on work hours and vacation schedules. Barry wants to preserve the friendship, but he also wants to treat all his employees fairly.

1. **What issues does Barry face?**

   - Both Barry and Robert must adjust to the shift in Barry's role from co-worker and friend to supervisor.

   - Barry needs to become comfortable with his new position of authority, and Robert must learn to respect Barry's position as supervisor.

   - If Barry gives preferential treatment to Robert, other employees will resent the fact that Barry is playing favorites.

   - Teamwork and motivation will suffer.

   - Workers will lose respect for both Barry and Robert.

   - If Robert persists in trying to trade on the friendship, Barry will have to ask himself whether Robert is a friend at all.

2. **How should Barry deal with this situation?**

   - At a private meeting in his office, Barry can explain to Robert that he is unable to approve Robert's requested work hours and vacation schedule because it would be unfair to other employees.

     - Barry can point out that he must treat all employees equitably, and ask for Robert's understanding and support.

     - Together they can look for acceptable alternatives that meet Robert's objectives in a way that is also fair to the others.

     - Barry can tell Robert that preferential treatment for him could harm team spirit and motivation, as well as damage Robert's relationships with his co-workers.

HANDOUT

Directions

Preserving the Friendship

Read the case study and answer the questions below. Be prepared to discuss your answers with your team, as well as with the entire class.

> While a rank-and-file employee, Barry became good friends with Robert, an employee he now supervises. Barry now thinks Robert is trying to take advantage of their friendship by asking for preferential treatment on work hours and vacation schedules. Barry wants to preserve the friendship, but he also wants to treat all his employees fairly.

1. What issues does Barry face?

2. How should Barry deal with this situation?

<table>
<tr><td>

</td><td>

Quality Is Below Standard

</td></tr>
<tr><td>

Description

</td><td>

This case is suitable for small group discussion, skill practice in trios, and front-of-the-room demonstration. The case addresses the issues of role shift, preserving friendships formed prior to promotion, supervisory authority and accountability, delegation, performance standards, and employee response to controls.

</td></tr>
<tr><td>

Objectives

</td><td>

As a result of this learning activity, participants will be able to:

- Anticipate problems new supervisors encounter.
- Develop strategies to deal with role shift.
- Explain standards of performance to employees.
- Redirect undesirable employee behavior.

</td></tr>
<tr><td>

Time

</td><td>

- 30 to 60 minutes.

</td></tr>
<tr><td>

Materials

</td><td>

- A copy of the case study, *Quality Is Below Standard* (p. 153), for each participant.
- A copy of the *Skill-Practice: Observer Checklist* (p. 154) for each observer if the case is used as an optional skill-practice exercise.

</td></tr>
<tr><td>

Procedure

</td><td>

1. Using information in the One-Day Training Plan (pp. 75-79), give a short lecture on challenges new supervisors face as they make the transition from operating employee to a member of the management team. Place special emphasis on role shift and controlling the work. (7 minutes)

2. Distribute the case study. Give participants four minutes to read the case and answer the accompanying questions. (6 minutes)

3. Assign participants to teams of three and give them five minutes to discuss the case and develop team answers to the questions. Tell teams to select a spokesperson to report on the discussion. (6 minutes)

4. Have teams give their reports. Look for answers that make the points listed after each question in the facilitator's copy of the activity. (5 minutes)

5. Summarize the discussion and conclude the activity. (3 minutes)

</td></tr>
</table>

Skill-Practice Option

1. Follow previous instructions one through four. (30 minutes)

2. Explain that it is as important for supervisors to practice their skills in a classroom learning laboratory as it is for an athlete to practice on the playing field. For that reason, the next learning activity is a skill practice. (3 minutes)

3. Assign participants to groups of three. Explain that one person is to practice the supervisor's part, while another practices the employee's part. The third person is the observer and timekeeper. If there are four in a group, the fourth person serves as an observer, also. Distribute one Skill-Practice Observer Checklist to each observer. Observers are to use these checklists to help them observe and give feedback. (3 minutes)

4. Allow three minutes for the skill practice and another three minutes for observer feedback and discussion by the parties. It is important for the individuals practicing the employee and supervisor's parts to discuss their feelings about the exercise. (6 minutes)

5. Conclude the exercise by asking each group for one insight they gained from the skill practice. (7 minutes)

Front-of-the-Room Demonstration Option

Select two participants to demonstrate the meeting between the supervisor and employee for the class. Afterward, ask the "supervisor" and the "employee" to describe their feelings, what they thought they did well, and what they would do differently. Ask the observers to give feedback as well.

A variation on the front-of-the-room demonstration is to stop the demonstration after three minutes. Discuss the progress made and the feelings experienced by the "supervisor" and the "employee." Then start a second round with two new players who continue the practice where the first two left off. At the end of the second round, discuss progress and feelings.

Facilitator's Copy With Answers

(Note: This case study can also be used as a skill practice.)

Read the case study and answer the questions below. Be prepared to discuss your answers with your team, as well as with the entire class.

> Recently Diane was selected to head the branch where she had worked for two years. Over that period, Diane socialized frequently with co-worker, Nancy. Diane values her friendship with Nancy. Three times since being promoted, Diane has met with Nancy to discuss a work project that is not proceeding according to plan. Each time Nancy has thrown a tantrum and has accused Diane of picking on her.
>
> Today Diane is meeting with Nancy once again to discuss the project, which is two weeks behind schedule.

1. **What issues are involved?**

   - Diane's role shift from peer to supervisor.

   - Diane's authority to delegate and control the work.

   - Diane and Nancy's friendship.

   - Treating co-workers (including your supervisor) with respect.

   - Meeting project deadlines.

2. **How should Diane open the meeting?**

   - State the purpose of the meeting.

   - Summarize their prior agreement.

3. **What topics should Diane discuss with Nancy?**

   - Project status, new time estimates.

   - Resources Nancy needs to complete the project.

   - Impact of delays on the work unit.

   - Consequences of failure to meet the schedule.

Facilitator's Copy (cont.)

4. **How should Diane respond to Nancy's tantrums?**

   - Remain calm.

   - Paraphrase the facts that Nancy states and acknowledge the feelings that she exhibits.

   - Set limits on Nancy's behavior.

   - Tell Nancy that she is responsible for meeting the schedule. Diane is accountable to upper management for the project. So, they need to revise the schedule.

5. **How should Diane close the meeting?**

   - Document their understanding in writing.

   - Ask Nancy to describe their agreement.

   - Remind Nancy of the consequences of not living up to the agreement.

   - Let Nancy know that the choice is hers.

   - Express confidence in Nancy's ability.

Notes

   - _____
   - _____
   - _____
   - _____
   - _____
   - _____
   - _____
   - _____
   - _____
   - _____
   - _____
   - _____
   - _____
   - _____
   - _____
   - _____

HANDOUT

Directions

Quality Is Below Standard

Read the case study and answer the questions below. Be prepared to discuss your answers with your team, as well as with the entire class.

> Recently Diane was selected to head the branch where she had worked for two years. Over that period, Diane socialized frequently with co-worker, Nancy. Diane values her friendship with Nancy. Three times since being promoted, Diane has met with Nancy to discuss a work project that is not proceeding according to plan. Each time Nancy has thrown a tantrum and has accused Diane of picking on her.
>
> Today Diane is meeting with Nancy once again to discuss the project, which is two weeks behind schedule.

1. **What issues are involved?**

2. **How should Diane open the meeting?**

3. **What topics should Diane discuss with Nancy?**

4. **How should Diane respond to Nancy's tantrums?**

5. **How should Diane close the meeting?**

<u>HANDOUT</u>

Directions

Skill-Practice: Observer Checklist

During the skill practice, watch for the six behaviors listed below. Place a check mark in the appropriate space to indicate whether or not the individual used the behavior listed. Give examples when possible.

Yes   **No**   **Behavior**

_____   _____   1. Did the supervisor describe the problem using specific examples?

_____   _____   2. Did the supervisor ask for the employee's views?

_____   _____   3. Did the supervisor paraphrase the employee's comments to be sure he/she understood the employee correctly?

_____   _____   4. Did the supervisor probe for additional information?

_____   _____   5. Did the supervisor and employee engage in joint problem solving?

_____   _____   6. Did the supervisor ask the employee to summarize their understanding?

TRAINER'S NOTES

Ignoring the Chain of Command

Description

This case is suitable for small group discussion, skill practice in trios, and front-of-the-room demonstration. The case addresses the issues of establishing supervisory power and authority, and of dealing with challenges to authority.

Objectives

As a result of this activity, participants will be able to:

- Anticipate problems new supervisors encounter.

- Develop strategies to establish authority.

- Develop strategies for dealing with challenges to authority.

Time

- 30 to 60 minutes.

Materials

- A copy of the case study, *Ignoring the Chain of Command* (p. 159), for each participant.

- A copy of the *Skill-Practice Observer Checklist* (p. 154) for each observer if the case is used as an optional skill-practice exercise.

Procedure

1. Using information in the One-Day Training Plan (pp. 75-79), give a short lecture on challenges new supervisors face as they make the transition from operating employee to a member of the management team. (7 minutes)

2. Distribute the case study. Give participants four minutes to read the case and answer the accompanying questions. (6 minutes)

3. Assign participants to teams of three and give them five minutes to discuss the case and answer the questions. Tell teams to select a spokesperson to report on the discussion. (6 minutes)

4. Have teams give their reports. Look for answers that make the points listed after each question in the facilitator's copy of the learning activity. (5 minutes)

5. Summarize the discussion and conclude the activity. (3 minutes)

Skill-Practice Option

1. Follow previous instructions one through four. (30 minutes)

2. Explain that it is as important for supervisors to practice their skills in a classroom learning laboratory as it is for an athlete to practice on the playing field. For that reason, the next learning activity is a skill practice. (3 minutes)

3. Assign participants to groups of three. Explain that one person is to practice the supervisor's part, while another practices the employee's part. The third person is the observer and timekeeper. If there are four in a group, the fourth person serves as an observer, also. Distribute one *Skill-Practice Observer Checklist* to each observer. Observers are to use these checklists to help them observe and give feedback. (3 minutes)

4. Allow three minutes for the skill practice and another three minutes for observer feedback and discussion by the parties. It is important for the individuals practicing the employee and supervisor's parts to discuss their feelings about the exercise. (6 minutes)

5. Conclude the exercise by asking each group for one insight they gained from the skill practice. (7 minutes)

Front-of-the-Room Demonstration Option

Select two participants to demonstrate the meeting between the supervisor and employee for the class. Afterward, ask the "supervisor" and the "employee" to describe their feelings, what they did well, and what they could do differently. Ask the observers to give feedback, as well.

A variation is to stop the demonstration after three minutes. Discuss the progress made and the feelings experienced by the "supervisor" and the "employee." Then start a second round with two new players who continue the practice where the first two left off. At the end of the second round, discuss progress and feelings.

Facilitator's Copy With Answers

Directions

(Note: This case study can also be used as a skill practice.)

Read the case study and answer the questions below. Be prepared to discuss your answers with your team, as well as with the entire class.

> Carla is a newly appointed branch head. She was selected for this position over Phil, whom she now supervises. Carla has more experience in the field than Phil. Nevertheless, Phil is outspoken in telling others he is better qualified for the position because he holds a master's degree while Carla has a bachelor's degree. Twice when Phil has needed a supervisory decision, he has gone directly to Carla's supervisor, Russ. In each case, Russ has met with Phil, made a decision, and then advised Carla.

1. **What issues does Carla face?**

   - Phil is challenging her authority and her qualifications.

   - Carla wants to retain the respect of the other employees that report to her.

   - Russ is undermining her authority by making decisions.

2. **How should Carla approach Russ?**

   - Ask Russ why he agreed to meet with Phil and give him a decision without involving Carla.

   - Explain to Russ how his behavior affects Carla's ability to manage the group.

   - Ask Russ to direct employees to her in the future.

   - Alternatively, ask him to take the matter under advisement, consult with her, and let her deal with her direct reports on the matter.

Facilitator's Copy (cont.)

3. **How should Carla approach Phil?**

   - Carla's approach to Phil will depend on whether Russ agrees to direct employees to her in the future.

   - Meet with Phil and explain that in the future both she and Russ will expect him to respect the chain of command and go to Carla for decisions.

   - Let Phil know that his statements about her lack of credentials inhibit teamwork and productivity, and ask that he refrain from making such comments.

   - Ask him what his career goals are and tell him that she is committed to helping all her employees develop on the job so that they will be qualified for career opportunities.

   - Ask for his help and support.

Notes

- _____
- _____
- _____
- _____
- _____
- _____
- _____
- _____
- _____
- _____
- _____
- _____
- _____
- _____
- _____
- _____
- _____
- _____
- _____

<u>H</u>ANDOUT

Directions

Ignoring the Chain of Command

Read the case study and answer the questions below. Be prepared to discuss your answers with your team, as well as with the entire class.

> Carla is a newly appointed branch head. She was selected for this position over Phil, whom she now supervises. Carla has more experience in the field than Phil. Nevertheless, Phil is outspoken in telling others he is better qualified for the position because he holds a master's degree while Carla has a bachelor's degree. Twice when Phil has needed a supervisory decision, he has gone directly to Carla's supervisor, Russ. In each case, Russ has met with Phil, made a decision, and then advised Carla.

1. **What issues does Carla face?**

2. **How should Carla approach Russ?**

3. **How should Carla approach Phil?**

Going Through the Work Orders

Description

This learning activity is designed to give participants practice in planning and organizing work.

Objectives

As a result of this activity, participants will be able to:

- Organize work.

- Use a mathematical planning formula to estimate how long a project will take to complete.

- Assign tasks to appropriate workers.

- Be alert to how stereotyping can influence the way in which work is assigned.

Time

- 50 minutes.

Materials

- Copies of the case study, *Going Through Work Orders* (p. 164-166) for each participant.

- Flipchart pad and stand, felt-tip marking pens, and masking tape.

Procedure

1. Introduce the learning activity by reviewing the objectives. Distribute copies of the case and ask participants to read it and answer the discussion questions. (10 minutes)

2. Assign participants to teams of three to four people. Tell the teams they have twelve minutes to develop team answers to the discussion questions and an additional seven minutes to create a chart that illustrates their solution. (20 minutes)

3. While the teams are working, distribute chart paper, marking pens, and masking tape.

4. Have a spokesperson from each team explain its solution and give the rationale. Look for answers that make the points listed after each question in the facilitator's copy of the activity. (10 minutes)

5. Summarize the responses and conclude the activity. (5 minutes)

Facilitator's Copy With Answers

> Jim supervises three laborers: Scott, Anne, and Todd. The ability to lift 30 pounds is a job qualification. Scott, formerly a carpenter, is 5-feet, 7-inches tall and weighs 145 pounds. Anne is 6-feet tall, 155 pounds, and lifts weights. Anne has worked for a moving company. Todd is 6-feet, 2-inches tall and weighs 190 pounds. Todd types 60 words per minute and previously worked in customer service.
>
> Jim and his crew are located in Building 3.

Today's Work Orders

Today Jim received the following work orders:

- Move six file cabinets from the second floor of Building 6 to the first floor of Building 10. Building 6 does not have an elevator.

- Set up and take down chairs and tables for a meeting of thirty-five people that will take place between 1:00 p.m. and 2:00 p.m. in the Building 1 fourth-floor conference room. The set-up is classroom style, with a facilitator's table, video player, monitor, overhead projector, and screen in the front. Each collapsible rectangular table seats three people. Tables and chairs are kept in a storeroom near the conference room. The audiovisual equipment must be obtained from and returned to the A/V department on the first floor of Building 6.

- One hundred boxes of paper weighing 25 pounds each need to be moved from the Building 10 loading dock to a supply area on the third floor of Building 1. Building 1 has a freight elevator.

  The unit secretary is on leave; so, the phones and office need to be covered.

Work Area Map

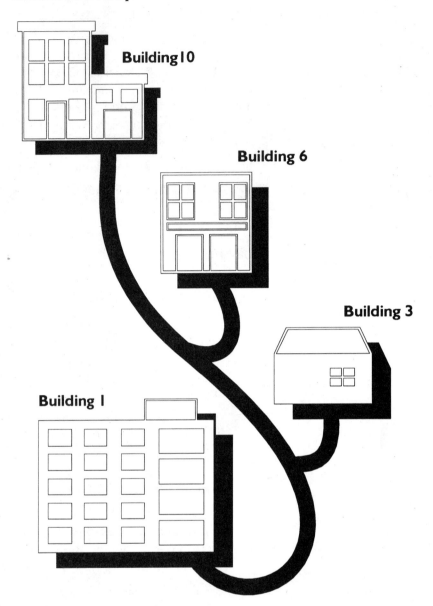

Travel Times

From	To	Elapsed Time
Building 1	Building 3	6 minutes
Building 3	Building 6	8 minutes
Building 6	Building 10	10 minutes

Discussion Questions

1. In what sequence should the jobs be performed? Why?

Jim can assign the work in a variety of ways. Those most commonly suggested by participants are:

- Have two people move file cabinets and a third set up the conference room. Then all three move the boxes of paper. Jim stays at the office to answer phones.

- Scott, Todd, and Anne work as a team on all the assignments. Jim answers the office phones.

- Two workers move the file cabinets first, and then unload the paper. The third worker sets up the conference room, and then staffs the office while Jim inspects completed work.

2. What jobs should Jim assign to which employees? Why?

- Jim should select the best qualified person for the assignment.

- Work should be assigned equitably.

- If participants suggest that Jim go out on the work party, point out that his job is to manage, not to do the actual work unless there is an emergency or unless he is a "working supervisor."

- If there were an unanticipated typing job that had to be completed by close of business, then Todd could staff the office and Jim could go out with the crew.

3. What is the estimated time, including travel, to complete each work order?

- Calculate the Estimated Time

  Take an optimistic, pessimistic, and most likely estimate, and then apply the following formula to calculate the estimated time:

$$\frac{\text{Optimistic} + \text{Pessimistic} + 4\ (\text{Most Likely})}{6} = \text{Estimated Time}$$

  Estimates will vary depending on how the work is structured. As participants are calculating their estimates, check their answers to be sure they are applying the formula correctly. A few will be confused about how to calculate the weighted average using four times the most likely estimate. They must always divide by six (optimistic = 1, pessimistic = 1, four times the most likely = 4; 1+1+4 = 6).

<u>HANDOUT</u>

Going Through the Work Orders

Jim supervises three laborers: Scott, Anne, and Todd. The ability to lift 30 pounds is a job qualification. Scott, formerly a carpenter, is 5-feet, 7-inches tall and weighs 145 pounds. Anne is 6-feet tall, 155 pounds, and lifts weights. Anne has worked for a moving company. Todd is 6-feet, 2-inches tall and weighs 190 pounds. Todd types 60 words per minute and previously worked in customer service.

Jim and his crew are located in Building 3.

Today's Work Orders

Today Jim received the following work orders:

- Move six file cabinets from the second floor of Building 6 to the first floor of Building 10. Building 6 does not have an elevator.

- Set up and take down chairs and tables for a meeting of thirty-five people that will take place between 1:00 p.m. and 2:00 p.m. in the Building 1 fourth-floor conference room. The set-up is classroom style, with a facilitator's table, video player, monitor, overhead projector, and screen in the front. Each collapsible rectangular table seats three people. Tables and chairs are kept in a storeroom near the conference room. The audiovisual equipment must be obtained from and returned to the A/V department on the first floor of Building 6.

- One hundred boxes of paper weighing 25 pounds each need to be moved from the Building 10 loading dock to a supply area on the third floor of Building 1. Building 1 has a freight elevator.

  The unit secretary is on leave; so, the phones and office need to be covered.

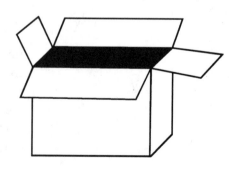

Work Area Map

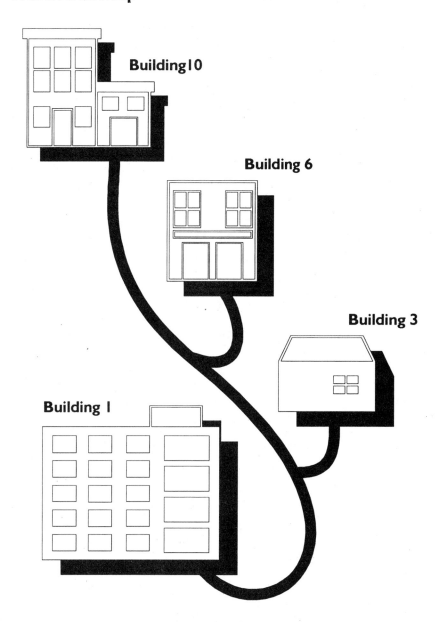

Travel Times

From	To	Elapsed Time
Building 1	Building 3	6 minutes
Building 3	Building 6	8 minutes
Building 6	Building 10	10 minutes

<u>HANDOUT</u>

Discussion Questions

1. In what sequence should the jobs be performed? Why?

2. What jobs should Jim assign to which employees? Why?

3. What is the estimated time, including travel, to complete each work order?

Take an optimistic, pessimistic, and most likely estimate, and then apply the following formula to calculate the estimated time:

$$\frac{\text{Optimistic} + \text{Pessimistic} + 4 \text{ (Most Likely)}}{6} = \text{Estimated Time}$$

Delegation Planning

Description

This learning activity is designed to allow participants to plan a delegation, practice delegating the assignment, and receive feedback during the workshop.

Time

- 40 minutes.

Materials

- One copy of the *Delegation Planning Worksheet* (p. 168) for each participant.

- Two copies of the *Delegation Skill-Practice Observer Checklist* (p. 169) for each participant.

Procedure

1. Tell participants the next learning activity will give them an opportunity to plan the delegation of an assignment that they want performed, as well as to practice actually delegating the assignment to the employee. Ask participants to think of a task that they will delegate when they return to work. (If someone cannot think of an assignment, suggest using a task they want performed at home. They can also use a task they have delegated in the past.) Distribute the *Delegation Planning Worksheet* and the *Delegation Skill-Practice Observer Checklist*. (4 minutes)

2. Have participants plan the task using the *Delegation Planning Worksheet*. (5 minutes)

3. Assign participants to groups of three for skill practice. Explain that there will be three skill-practice rounds so that each person can practice delegating an assignment to an employee, who will be played by another member of the trio. The third person serves as the observer. Show the overhead transparency, *Round-Robin Skill-Practice* (p. 223), to illustrate how the round-robin skill practice works. At the conclusion of each round, the observer is to give feedback using the *Delegation Skill-Practice: Observer Checklist*. (4 minutes)

4. Do the skill practice. (15 minutes)

5. Call time on the skill practice and ask each team to summarize what they did and what they learned. (10 minutes)

6. Summarize the group comments and conclude the activity. (2 minutes)

<u>HANDOUT</u>   **Delegation Planning Worksheet**

1. Describe the task you want to delegate.

2. List the subtasks involved in completing the main task.

3. Describe the end result.

4. What is the completion date?

5. What is the budget?

6. Describe any unusual constraints.

7. To which employee will you delegate this task?

8. On a scale of 1 through 5, with 1 being lowest and 5 being highest, rate the employee's readiness to perform the task.

Low				High
1	2	3	4	5

9. How do you know that the employee can perform the job to the standard?

10. How does this task relate to other priorities you have given the employee?

11. What alternative methods do you have for accomplishing this task?

Delegation Skill-Practice: Observer Checklist

Directions   Observe the person who is practicing delegating an assignment. Place a check mark in the appropriate space to indicate whether or not the individual used the behavior listed. Give examples when possible.

Yes	No	Behavior
_____	_____	**1.** Gave background on the assignment.
_____	_____	**2.** Explained why the employee was selected.
_____	_____	**3.** Described advantages for the employee.
_____	_____	**4.** Described desired outcome, including completion date.
_____	_____	**5.** Involved employee in defining scope of work, describing results, setting the schedule, selecting work methods, establishing controls, and deciding how performance will be measured.
_____	_____	**6.** Described extent of authority being delegated.
_____	_____	**7.** Described budget and other resources available.
_____	_____	**8.** Asked employee to describe his or her understanding.
_____	_____	**9.** Encouraged questions.
_____	_____	**10.** Offered support.

Giving Instructions

Description

This learning activity is designed to provide skill practice in giving and following instructions, as well as to illustrate the importance of giving clear instructions. It is intended to accompany a short lecture on interpersonal communication, delegation, giving and following instructions, or coaching and training employees.

Objectives

As a result of this activity, participants will be able to:

- Describe effective techniques for giving instructions.

- Describe effective techniques for listening to and following instructions.

Time

- 45 minutes.

Materials

- One large, colorful athletic shoe with the lace removed. (For hygienic reasons, use an athletic shoe that never has been worn.)

- One shoe lace.

- One copy of the background sheet, *Extra Mile Athletic Shoes: Supervisor* (p. 171) for the participant that plays the role of the supervisor.

- One copy of the background sheet, *Extra Mile Athletic Shoes: Employee* (p. 172) for the participant that plays the part of the employee.

- Copies of the background sheet *Extra Mile Athletic Shoes: Observer* (p. 173) for all participants except the employees playing the supervisor and employee.

Procedure

For directions and a facilitator's script, please see the One-Hour Supervision Workshop on "Giving Instructions" (pp. 111-122).

Variations on this activity

1. Instead of having a front-of-the-room demonstration, divide the class into teams of four. Have each team perform the skill practice, with one member acting as the supervisor, a second as the employee, and the third and fourth as observers. Have each team discuss the learning activity as a small group, using the questions on the worksheets as the focus of discussion. Then ask each team to report to the entire class on what members learned from the activity.

2. Instead of an athletic shoe, use other articles of clothing; for instance, have one person teach another how to tie a necktie or put on a jacket.

Extra Mile Athletic Shoes: Supervisor

**Background
for the supervisor**

> You supervise a unit at Straight Laced Services that is responsible for lacing and tying athletic shoes before they are shipped to Extra Mile Athletic Shoes, a chain that stakes its reputation on extra touches such as having all shoes laced and tied when customers open the shoe box. If customers find an unlaced or untied pair of shoes, the store discounts the merchandise by 10 percent. Extra Mile Athletic Shoes, a very important account for your company, expects all shoes to be laced and tied perfectly. The contract with the retail chain contains a penalty clause requiring Straight Laced Services to refund all charges for improperly laced and tied shoes.
>
> An employee with no prior experience lacing and tying athletic shoes has just reported to work. You must explain the assignment and teach the individual how to lace and tie the shoes to the quality standards expected by Extra Mile Athletic Shoes.

During the skill practice, be alert to the following considerations and be prepared to discuss them afterwards:

1. What difficulties are you having in giving directions? Why?

2. What techniques are working best?

3. What could you do differently?

<u>H</u>ANDOUT

Extra Mile Athletic Shoes: Employee

**Background
for the employee**

> You have just reported for your first day of work at Straight Laced Services and are meeting with your supervisor, who will explain your responsibilities. Your job is to lace and tie athletic shoes that will be shipped to Extra Mile Athletic Shoes. You have no prior experience lacing and tying shoes. During this exercise, follow the instructions given by your supervisor to the letter. If the supervisor asks, "Do you understand?" nod and say, "Yes."

During the skill practice, be alert to the following considerations and be prepared to discuss them afterward:

1. **What difficulties are you having in following the directions? Why?**

2. **What is the supervisor doing that is helping you to learn the task?**

3. **What else could the supervisor do to help you master the task more quickly or easily?**

4. **What could you have done to help the supervisor teach you the task?**

<u>H</u>ANDOUT   **Extra Mile Athletic Shoes: Observer**

**Background
for the supervisor**

You supervise a unit at Straight Laced Services that is responsible for lacing and tying athletic shoes before they are shipped to Extra Mile Athletic Shoes, a chain that stakes its reputation on extra touches such as having all shoes laced and tied when customers open the shoe box. If customers find an unlaced or untied pair of shoes, the store discounts the merchandise by 10 percent. Extra Mile Athletic Shoes, a very important account for your company, expects all shoes to be laced and tied perfectly. The contract with the retail chain contains a penalty clause requiring Straight Laced Services to refund all charges for improperly laced and tied shoes.

An employee with no prior experience lacing and tying athletic shoes has just reported to work. You must explain the assignment and teach the individual how to lace and tie the shoes to the quality standards expected by Extra Mile Athletic Shoes.

Background for the employee

You have just reported for your first day of work at Straight Laced Services and are meeting with your supervisor, who will explain your responsibilities. Your job is to lace and tie athletic shoes that will be shipped to Extra Mile Athletic Shoes. You have no prior experience lacing and tying shoes. During this exercise, follow the instructions given by your supervisor to the letter. If the supervisor asks, "Do you understand?" nod and say, "Yes."

Giving Instructions Skill-Practice: Observer Checklist

As you observe the skill practice, watch for the following:

 1. **What communications techniques does the supervisor use to help the employee learn the task?**

 2. **What behaviors does the supervisor use that make it more difficult for the employee to learn the task?**

 3. **What does the employee do to help the learning process?**

 4. **What does the employee do that inhibits the learning process?**

Chapter Nine:

Tools and Assessments

In this chapter, you will find tools and assessments for use during your supervision training sessions.

USING THE TOOLS AND ASSESSMENTS

Before each tool or assessment, you'll find instructions on its use. In cases where the facilitator needs sample answers to questions, an annotated facilitator's copy precedes the participants' version of the tool or assessment.

You can use them in two ways:

- Key them into your word processing system "as is" or customize them to suit your specific needs.

- Photocopy the tools and assessments you need from this book and use them "as is."

Self-Appraisal

Instructions

Description

This self-appraisal is designed to help nonsupervisors decide whether or not they are ready to become supervisors. The assessment is reprinted with permission from *What Every Supervisor Should Know*, Sixth Edition, by Lester R. Bittel and John W. Newstrom (New York: McGraw-Hill, 1990).

Objectives

As a result of completing this self-appraisal, participants will gain insight about:

- Whether they are ready to consider a career in management.

- Whether they should look to occupations other than management for a career.

- Whether they should continue their studies of management and supervision.

Time
- 30 to 60 minutes.

Equipment
- Overhead projector (optional).

Materials
- One copy per participant of:

  – *How Ready Are You to be a Supervisor?* (pp. 178-179).

  – *High-Performance Management Versus Low-Octane Management,*(p. 15).

  – *The Basics of Supervision* (p. 124).

  – *Management Levels* (pp. 125-126).

  – *Supervisory Job Knowledge* (p. 218).

  – *Management Skills* (p. 219).

Procedure

1. Present an overview of the basics of supervision using material in the One-Day Training Plan, (pp. 65-74). Show the overhead transparency, *Management Process*, (p. 214), to illustrate the process. Show the overhead transparency, *Management Levels*, (p. 215), to illustrate how supervisors fit into the management chain. Explain that effective management is crucial to organizational success in today's highly competitive global marketplace. Give some of the reasons cited in the Chapter 2 section, *High-Performance Management Versus Low-Octane Management*, (pp. 14-15), and distribute copies of that document. (10 minutes)

2. Introduce the self-appraisal. Explain that it will help participants assess their readiness to consider supervision as a career. Distribute the appraisal and explain how to score it. Ask participants to complete the self-appraisal. (7 minutes)

3. Circulate about the room to ensure that participants are scoring the self-appraisal correctly and to answer questions.

4. Call time and ask for questions or comments. Explain that many factors go into a career decision. The information gained from the self-appraisal is only one of many factors to be considered when making a career choice. (3 minutes)

5. Describe the knowledge and skills needed to be a supervisor, using material from the One-Day Training Plan. Show the overhead transparencies, *Supervisory Job Knowledge*, (p. 218), and *Management Skills*, (p. 219). Distribute paper copies of the transparencies. (5 minutes)

6. Close the session by telling participants that when making career choices, it's a good practice to learn as much as they can about careers that interest them. Point out that today everyone has learned about the functions of supervisors, as well as about the knowledge and skills required to be an effective supervisor. As a result, they are now better able to make more informed choices about their own future. Wish participants good luck in their future endeavors and adjourn the session. (3 minutes)

HANDOUT   How Ready Are You to Be a Supervisor?

Read each statement carefully. Then place a check mark in the column that most nearly matches your feeling about each statement. After completing this activity, check your answers using the scoring procedure that follows the list.

Agree	Disagree	Neither Agree nor Disagree	
___	___	___	1. I like to set my own goals and do things my own way.
___	___	___	2. I have a keen sensitivity to the interests of other people.
___	___	___	3. I see my work as a means only to an end, rather than as a main focus for my life.
___	___	___	4. When I know a job needs to be done well, I will do it myself.
___	___	___	5. I don't want to take the responsibility for someone else's work, good or bad.
___	___	___	6. I consider myself an attentive listener: I don't interrupt.
___	___	___	7. Given a fair chance, most people want to do a good job.
___	___	___	8. I live according to the rule of "better late than never."
___	___	___	9. When working with a group of other people on a project, I often find myself prodding them to get the job done.
___	___	___	10. I have a lot to learn about management and supervision.
___	___	___	11. Good employees work safely, obey the rules, and are willing to give a fair day's work.
___	___	___	12. My friends know that I won't criticize them when they come to me with their hard-luck stories.
___	___	___	13. People who break rules should be prepared to pay the penalty.
___	___	___	14. I like to show other people how to do things.
___	___	___	15. The thought of working overtime without extra pay seems extremely unfair.
___	___	___	16. Most of my bosses have been a hindrance rather than a help to me and my coworkers.
___	___	___	17. I consider myself to be a good explainer: I can make things clear to other people.
___	___	___	18. In handling my personal affairs, I rarely fall behind in what I set out to do.
___	___	___	19. When assessing a situation, I find that there is likely to be some good in it as well as the bad and the ugly.
___	___	___	20. When things go wrong, that's a sign that a problem needs to be solved rather than a person blamed.

Source: Lester R. Bittel and John W. Newstrom, *What Every Supervisor Should Know*, Sixth Edition, New York: McGraw-Hill, 1990. Adapted and reprinted with permission

Scoring

Give yourself one point for each of the following statements that you *agreed* with: 2, 6, 7, 9, 10, 11, 12, 13, 14, 17, 18, 19, 20. Give yourself one point for each of the following statements that you *disagreed* with: 1, 3, 4, 5, 8, 15, 16. There are no points for statements with which you neither agreed nor disagreed.

Agree		**Disagree**	
2.	_____	1.	_____
6.	_____	3.	_____
7.	_____	4.	_____
9.	_____	5.	_____
10.	_____	8.	_____
11.	_____	15.	_____
12.	_____	16.	_____
13.	_____		
14.	_____		
17.	_____		
18.	_____		
19.	_____		
20.	_____		

Total: _____   _____

Interpretation

If you scored between 15 and 20 points, you are ready to consider the pursuit of a supervisory position. If you scored between 9 and 14 points, you should try now to gain a fuller understanding of what a supervisory position entails. If you scored less than 9 points, it's probably wise to look to other occupations for a career. Do continue your studies of supervision, however, so that your working life will be made more fruitful from your understanding of the supervisors and managers with whom you will be associated.

Supervisory Roles Assessment

REFERENCE CONTEXT

The Supervisory Roles Assessment is used in conjunction with the following related materials and activities:

Topic: Basics of Supervision

Scripts: One-Day Workshop,
                      Modules 3 and 4, (pp. 65-79)

Handouts: Basics of Supervision, (p. 124)
                      Management Levels, (pp. 125-126)
                      Supervisory Roles, (p. 127)
                      Management Skills, (p. 219)
                      Challenges Facing New Supervisors,
                      (p. 220)

Overheads: Management Process, (p. 214)
                      Management Levels, (p. 215)
                      Supervisory Responsibilities, (p. 216)
                      Supervisory Roles, (p. 217)
                      Supervisory Job Knowledge, (p. 218)
                      Management Skills, (p. 219)
                      Challenges Facing New Supervisors,
                      (p. 220)

Learning Activities: He's Sinking Fast, (pp. 138-141)
                      Delivering Unpopular News,
                      (pp. 142-145)
                      Preserving the Friendship,
                      (pp. 146-148)
                      Quality Is Below Standard,
                      (pp. 149-153)
                      Ignoring the Chain of Command,
                      (p. 155-159)

The following *Supervisory Roles Assessment* consists of three distinct parts:

Part I   Gives participants practice in identifying supervisory roles.

Part II   Asks participants to apply general knowledge about supervisory roles to their specific situation by describing the roles that they play and the roles that others expect them to play.

Part III Helps participants analyze the similarities and differences between the roles they play and the roles others expect them to play. Then, they develop an action plan to address the differences.

Instructions

Objectives   As a result of this assessment, participants will be able to:

- Describe supervisory roles.
- Identify supervisory roles that they play.
- Describe roles that others expect them to play.
- Develop an action plan to address differences between how they view their roles and what others expect of them.

Time   • 60 minutes.

Equipment   • Overhead projector (optional).

Materials
- Copies of the *Supervisory Roles Assessment* for each participant (pp. 184-185).
- Copies of the handout *Supervisory Roles* for each participant (p. 127).

Procedure   Follow the directions in the One-Day Training Plan (pp. 53-81).

Option   Schedule a thirty-minute reinforcement session within seven to fourteen days. As you conclude this assessment, instruct participants to be prepared to report on the results of implementing their action plans when you meet again for the reinforcement session.

Sample answers

A. Situation	B. Possible Roles
1. Two employees are in conflict over how to perform an assignment.	• Referee • Teacher • Negotiator • Judge
2. An employee has personal problems.	• Counselor • Chaplain • Parent
3. Another department is trying to take over facilities and equipment that are currently assigned to the supervisor's department.	• Spokesperson • Gladiator • Negotiator
4. The team is developing a new process, product, or service.	• Team captain • Leader • Cheerleader • Spokesperson • Resource allocator
5. The supervisor represents the organization at a civic or professional meeting.	• Spokesperson

<u>HANDOUT</u>

Part I: Supervisory Roles Assessment

SUPERVISORY ROLES

Each day supervisors assume a variety of roles as they interact with others. A role is a character that the supervisor assumes in a particular situation, much like an actor plays a role in a film. Part 1 of this assessment gives you practice matching roles to situations. Part 2 gives you an opportunity to assess the roles you play, as well as the roles others expect you to play. Part 3 is an action plan that allows you to decide what steps you will take to address differences between how you view your roles and how others view your roles.

Directions

Typical situations are provided in Column A of the answer sheet below. In Column B, list the roles a supervisor could assume in each situation. Row 1, Column B is an example.

Answer sheet

A. Situation	B. Possible Roles
1. Two employees are in conflict over how to perform an assignment.	• Referee • Negotiator • Teacher
2. An employee has personal problems.	
3. Another department is trying to take over facilities and equipment that are currently assigned to the supervisor's department.	
4. The team is developing a new process, product, or service.	
5. The supervisor represents the organization at a civic or professional meeting.	

<u>H</u>ANDOUT   **Part II: What Roles Do You Play?**

Directions   In Column A of the answer sheet below, list situations that you
                      encounter at work. In Column B, list roles that you play in those
                      situations. In Column C, list roles that others expect you to play in
                      each situation.

Answer Sheet

A. Situation	B. Roles I Play	C. Roles Others Expect Me to Play
1.		
2.		
3.		

Part III: Action Planning

Directions

Answer questions 1 to 4. Then on the planning form, list actions you will take to address differences between how you view your roles and how others view your roles.

 1. **What similarities are there between the roles you play and the roles others expect you to play?**

 2. **What differences are there?**

 3. **How do you explain the differences?**

 4. **What will you do to address the differences?**

(Record your answers to this question on the Planning Form that appears on the following page.)

<u>**H**ANDOUT</u>   **Planning Form**

A. Action(s)	B. Target Date(s)	C. Result(s)

Planning Survey

REFERENCE CONTEXT

The Planning Survey is used in conjunction with the following related materials and activities:

Topic:	Planning
Scripts:	Half-Day Training Plan, (pp. 90-99)
Handouts:	Creating Goals and Objectives, (p. 128)
	Implementing a Plan, (p. 224)
Overheads:	Implementing a Plan, (p. 224)
Learning Activities:	Going Through the Work Orders, (pp. 160-163)
Tools and Assessments:	Workforce Trial Balance Planning, (pp. 191-193)
Reinforcement:	Workforce Trial Balance Planning, (pp. 191-193)

Instructions

Description

With this *Planning Survey*, participants first review typical planning tasks and consider whether they place appropriate emphasis on those tasks. Then they identify corrective actions that they will take when they return to the workplace. This survey can be used either to open or to close a session on planning.

Objectives

As a result of completing this planning survey, participants will be able to:

- Identify planning tasks that they perform.

- Assess whether they place appropriate emphasis on planning tasks.

- List actions that they will take when they return to the workplace to arrive at the appropriate balance between planning and other supervisory functions.

Time
- 35 minutes.

Equipment
- Overhead projector (optional).

Materials
- Copies of the *Planning Survey* for each participant (pp. 188-189).

Procedure

1. Using information in the Half-Day Training Plan, (pp. 83-110), and the overhead transparency, *Implementing a Plan*, (p. 224), give a brief overview of the planning function at the supervisory level. (5 minutes)

2. Introduce the *Planning Survey* and distribute copies. (3 minutes)

3. Review the directions and give participants ten minutes to complete the survey and create their action plans. (11 minutes)

4. Call time and ask for volunteers to list some of the tasks on which they spend too little time, along with some of their action steps. Then ask for volunteers to share tasks on which they spend too much time, along with action steps. (10 minutes)

5. Summarize the discussion and conclude the activity. (3 minutes)

<u>**HANDOUT**</u>   **Part I: Planning Survey**

Procedure

A list of tasks that supervisors perform when they are engaged in the planning function follows:

- **Step 1**

  If you perform a task, place a check mark in the box in front of the item.

- **Step 2**

  After each item, indicate whether the amount of time you devote to that planning task is too little, about right, or too much.

- **Step 3**

  Review the items where you indicated that you devote too little or too much time. Select between one and three of these items. On the Action Plan in Part II A and B, list the actions you will take to adjust the amount of time so that it is about right.

The amount of time I devote to this task is:

✓	Planning Tasks	Too Little	About Right	Too Much
	1. Develop work schedules.			
	2. Develop the budget.			
	3. Develop the vacation schedule.			
	4. Work with my upline manager to develop the unit's annual goals and objectives.			
	5. Work with my direct reports to develop their individual goals and objectives.			
	6. Work with my upline manager to develop my goals and objectives.			
	7. Develop the preventive maintenance schedule for equipment.			
	8. Develop annual training plans for each employee.			
	9. Make plans for acquisition of new equipment.			
	10. Think about where the work unit is going in relation to the goals of the enterprise.			
	11. Focus resources on activities that have the highest payoff.			
	12. Build a skilled, balanced work team that will meet the unit's future needs.			
	13. Plan to obtain materials, tools, and equipment in a timely manner.			
	14. Schedule operations to utilize machinery at optimum capacity.			
	15. Schedule operations to utilize people at full capacity.			

<u>HANDOUT</u>   **Part II: Action Plan**

A.   In the space below, list the steps you will take to place more emphasis on tasks to which you devote too little time.

Tasks to Which I Devote Too Little Time	Actions I Will Take to Improve the Situation	Target Date

B.   In the space below, list steps you will take to place less emphasis on tasks to which you devote too much time.

Tasks to Which I Devote Too Much Time	Actions I Will Take to Improve the Situation	Target Date

<u>**TRAINER'S NOTES**</u>   # Workforce Trial Balance Planning

---

REFERENCE CONTEXT

The Workforce Trial Balance Planning Worksheet is used in conjunction with the following related materials and activities:

Topic: Planning

Scripts: Half-Day Training Workshop, Modules 1 and 2, (pp. 90-99)

Handouts: Creating Goals and Objectives, (p. 128)

Implementing a Plan, (p. 224)

Overheads: Implementing a Plan, (p. 224)

Learning Activities: Going Through the Work Orders, (pp. 160-167)

Tools and Assessments: Planning Survey, (pp. 188-191)

Instructions

Description

This *Workforce Trial Balance Worksheet* is a planning tool that supervisors can use to estimate how many workers they will need during a given time period. The worksheet is reprinted with permission from *What Every Supervisor Should Know*, Sixth Edition, by Lester R. Bittel and John W. Newstrom (New York: McGraw-Hill, 1990).

Objectives

As a result of using this worksheet, participants will be able to:

- Estimate the number of workers needed to meet the present workload.

- Estimate the number of workers needed at the end of a given period.

Time
- 30 to 60 minutes.

Equipment
- Calculators.

   If participants will complete the worksheet during the workshop, ask them to bring calculators.

Materials
- Copies of the *Workforce Trial Balance Planning Worksheet* for each participant (p. 193).

Procedure

1. At the conclusion of a lecture on planning, distribute copies of the worksheet to each participant.

2. Tell participants that this worksheet will help them to estimate the number of workers they will need at the beginning and at the end of a given work period. Most participants will have to research their office records before they can complete the worksheet.

Option

Schedule a thirty- to sixty-minute reinforcement session within seven to fourteen days after the workshop. For homework, ask participants to complete their worksheets and bring them to the reinforcement session for discussion.

<u>HANDOUT</u>   **Workforce Trial Balance Planning Worksheet**[*]

Dept: _____ Period: from _____ to _____ .

1. Number of workers needed to meet present workload:
    Direct
    Indirect   _____
        Subtotal   _____
                                                                  _____

2. Number of additional workers to allow for:
    a. Scheduled workday losses
        Holidays   _____
        Vacations   _____
            Subtotal
    b. Unscheduled workday losses   _____
        Sickness and other excused absence   _____
        Unexcused absences   _____
            Subtotal   _____

3. Total number of workers needed to staff department at beginning of period
    (subtotal line 1 + subtotal 2a + subtotal 2b):   _____

4. Number of workers to be added during the period to:
    a. Replace anticipated workforce losses
        Retirements   _____
        Promotions and transfers   _____
        Discharges   _____
        Leaves of absence   _____
            Subtotal   _____
    b. Replace unanticipated workforce losses†
        Resignations and quits   _____
        Disabilities   _____
        Deaths   _____
            Subtotal   _____

5. Total number of employees needed to replace losses during
    the period (subtotal 4a + 4b):   _____

6. Number of employees needed to meet anticipated change in
    department workload during the period:
    a. Additions to meet increase in workload   _____
    b. Less: Removals to allow for decrease in workload   (—)   _____

7. Total number of workers needed at end of period
    Number on line 3   _____
    Number on line 5   _____
    Number on line 6a or b (+ or —)   _____
        Total   _____

*   All entries are in number of workers.
†   If no past records are available, use 5% of the total on line 1.

Source: Lester R. Bittel and John W. Newstrom, *What Every Supervisor Should Know*,
Sixth Edition, New York: McGraw-Hill, 1990. Reprinted with permission.

Organizing Survey

REFERENCE CONTEXT

The Organizing Survey is used in conjunction with the following related materials and activities:

Topic: Organizing

Scripts: Half-Day Workshop, (pp. 100-110)

Handouts: Key Organizing Questions, (p. 129)

Learning Activities: Going Through Work Orders,
                          (pp. 160-166)

Instructions

Description

With this *Organizing Survey*, participants first review typical organizing tasks and consider whether they place appropriate emphasis on those tasks. Then they identify corrective actions they will take when they return to the workplace. This survey can be used either to open or to close a session on organizing.

Objectives

As a result of completing this *Organizing Survey*, participants will be able to:

- Identify organizing tasks that they perform.

- Assess whether they place appropriate emphasis on organizing tasks.

- List actions they will take when they return to the workplace to arrive at the appropriate balance between organizing and other supervisory functions.

Time
- 35 minutes.

Equipment
- None.

Materials
- Copies of the *Organizing Survey* for each participant (pp. 196-197).

Procedure

1. Using information in the Half-Day Training Plan, (pp. 83-110), and in the handout *Key Organizing Questions*, (p. 129), give a brief overview of the organizing function. (5 minutes)

2. Introduce the *Organizing Survey* and distribute copies. (3 minutes)

3. Review the directions and give participants ten minutes to complete the survey and create their action plans. (11 minutes)

4. Call time and ask for volunteers to list some of the tasks on which they spend too little time, along with some of their action steps. Then ask for volunteers to share tasks on which they spend too much time, along with action steps. (10 minutes)

5. Summarize the discussion and conclude the activity. (3 minutes)

Part I: Organizing Survey

Procedure

A list of tasks that supervisors perform when they are engaged in the organizing function follows.

- **Step 1**

  If you perform a task, place a check mark in the box in front of the item.

- **Step 2**

  After each item, indicate whether the amount of time you devote to that organizing task is too little, about right, or too much.

- **Step 3**

  Review the items where you indicated that you devote too little or too much time. Select between one and three of these items. On the Action Plan in Part II A and B, list the actions that you will take to adjust the amount of time so that it is about right.

<u>HANDOUT</u>   **Part II: Action Plan**

A.   In the space below, list the steps you will take to place more emphasis on tasks to which you devote too little time.

Tasks to Which I Devote Too Little Time	Actions I Will Take to Improve the Situation	Target Date

B.   In the space below, list steps you will take to place less emphasis on tasks to which you devote too much time.

Tasks to Which I Devote Too Much Time	Actions I Will Take to Improve the Situation	Target Date

Leading Survey

REFERENCE CONTEXT

The Leading Survey is used in conjunction with the following related materials and activities:

Topic:	Leading
Background:	(pp. 14-25, 28-29)
Scripts:	One-Day Workshop, Module 2, (pp 65-74)
Handouts:	Leading, (p. 131) Leadership and Motivation, (p. 132)
Learning Actitivies:	Delivering Unpopular News, (pp. 142-145)

Instructions

Description

With this *Leading Survey*, participants first review typical leading tasks and consider whether they place appropriate emphasis on those tasks. Then they identify corrective actions that they will take when they return to the workplace. This survey can be used either to open or to close a session on leading.

Objectives

As a result of completing this survey, participants will be able to:

- Identify leading tasks that they perform.

- Assess whether they place appropriate emphasis on leading tasks.

- List actions that they will take when they return to the workplace to arrive at the appropriate balance between leading and other supervisory functions.

Time
- 35 minutes.

Equipment
- None.

Materials
- Copies of the *Leading Survey* for each participant (pp. 200-202).

Procedure

1. Using information in the handouts, *Leading* (p. 131) and *Leadership and Motivation* (p. 132), give a brief overview of the leading function. (5 minutes)

2. Introduce the *Leading Survey* and distribute copies. (3 minutes)

3. Review the directions and give participants ten minutes to complete the survey and create their action plans. (11 minutes)

4. Call time and ask for volunteers to list some of the tasks on which they spend too little time, along with some of their action steps. Then ask for volunteers to share tasks on which they spend too much time, along with action steps. (10 minutes)

5. Summarize the discussion and conclude the activity. (3 minutes)

<u>**HANDOUT**</u>   **Part I: Leading Survey**

Procedure

A list of tasks that supervisors perform when they are engaged in the leading function follows.

*   **Step 1**

    If you perform a task, place a check mark in the box in front of the item.

*   **Step 2**

    After each item, indicate whether the amount of time you devote to that leading task is too little, about right, or too much.

*   **Step 3**

    Review the items where you indicated that you devote too little or too much. Select between one and three of these items. On the Action Plan in Part II A and B, list actions that you will take to adjust the amount of time so that it is about right.

The amount of time I devote to this task is:

✓	Leading Tasks	Too Little	About Right	Too Much
	1. Communicate a vision.			
	2. Inspire a sense of mission in others.			
	3. Embody organizational values and instill them in others.			
	4. Treat others with respect.			
	5. Represent followers' points of view to others.			
	6. Keep the work unit's activities aligned with the goals of the enterprise.			
	7. Let team members know what's going on in the organization.			
	8. Stay current in my profession or trade, and help others to do this also.			
	9. Spot trends, assess threats and opportunities, and share the information with others.			
	10. Bring about change.			
	11. Encourage creativity and innovation.			
	12. Sell ideas.			
	13. Foster desired behavior in others by rewarding their efforts.			
	14. Practice good personal time-management habits.			

<u>**HANDOUT**</u>   **Part II: Action Plan**

A.   In the space below, list the steps you will take to place more emphasis on tasks to which you devote too little time.

Tasks to Which I Devote Too Little Time	Actions I Will Take to Improve the Situation	Target Date

B.   In the space below, list steps you will take to place less emphasis on tasks to which you devote too much time.

Tasks to Which I Devote Too Much Time	Actions I Will Take to Improve the Situation	Target Date

Controlling Survey

> ## REFERENCE CONTEXT
>
> The Controlling Survey is used in conjunction with the following related materials and activities:
>
> | | |
> |---|---|
> | **Topic:** | Controlling |
> | **Scripts:** | One-Day Workshop, Modules 3 and 4, (pp. 65-79) |
> | **Handouts:** | Controlling, (p. 133) |
> | | The Control Process, (p. 134) |
> | **Learning Activities:** | Delivering Unpopular News, (pp. 142-145) |
> | | Quality is Below Standard, (pp. 150-154) |
> | | Ignoring the Chain of Command, (pp. 155-159) |

Instructions

Description

With this *Controlling Survey*, participants first review typical controlling tasks and consider whether they place appropriate emphasis on those tasks. Then they identify corrective actions that they will take when they return to the workplace. This survey can be used either to open or to close a session on controlling.

Objectives

As a result of completing this survey, participants will be able to:

- Identify controlling tasks that they perform.

- Assess whether they place appropriate emphasis on controlling tasks.

- List actions that they will take when they return to the workplace to arrive at the appropriate balance between controlling and other supervisory functions.

Time
- 35 minutes.

Equipment
- None.

Materials
- Copies of the *Controlling Survey* for each participant (pp. 205-206).

Procedure

1. Using information in the participant handouts, *Controlling*, (p. 133), and *The Control Process*, (p. 134), give a brief overview of the controlling function. (5 minutes)

2. Introduce the *Controlling Survey* and distribute copies. (3 minutes)

3. Review the directions and give participants ten minutes to complete the survey and create their action plans. (11 minutes)

4. Call time and ask for volunteers to list some of the tasks on which they spend too little time, along with some of their action steps. Then ask for volunteers to share tasks on which they spend too much time, along with action steps. (10 minutes)

5. Summarize the discussion and conclude the activity. (3 minutes)

Part I: Controlling Survey

Procedure

A list of tasks that supervisors perform when they are engaged in the controlling function follows:

- **Step 1**

  If you perform a task, place a check mark in the box in front of the item.

- **Step 2**

  After each item, indicate whether the amount of time you devote to that controlling task is too little, about right, or too much.

- **Step 3**

  Review the items where you indicated that you devote too little or too much time. Select between one and three of these items. On the Action Plan in Part II A and B, list actions that you will take to adjust the amount of time so that it is about right.

The amount of time I devote to this task is:

✓	Controlling Tasks	Too Little	About Right	Too Much
	1. Communicate performance standards to employees.			
	2. Place limits on an employee's authority.			
	3. Observe employee work habits and methods.			
	4. Give employees day-to-day performance feedback.			
	5. Conduct periodic formal performance reviews.			
	6. Praise or otherwise reward quality work.			
	7. Discipline an employee for violating a rule.			
	8. Establish budgets.			
	9. Review the unit's expenditures regularly to stay within budget.			
	10. Make sure accepted safety practices are being followed.			
	11. Check production records to see if an acceptable quantity of work is being turned out on schedule.			
	12. See if preventive equipment maintenance is being performed regularly.			
	13. Investigate an equipment malfunction.			
	14. Make sure that materials aren't wasted.			
	15. Make sure that tools aren't stolen.			

<u>HANDOUT</u>   **Part II: Action Plan**

A.   In the space below, list the steps you will take to place more emphasis on tasks to which you devote too little time.

Tasks to Which I Devote Too Little Time	Actions I Will Take to Improve the Situation	Target Date

B.   In the space below, list steps you will take to place less emphasis on tasks to which you devote too much time.

Tasks to Which I Devote Too Much Time	Actions I Will Take to Improve the Situation	Target Date

Skill-Application Planning

REFERENCE CONTEXT

The Skill Application Planner is used in conjunction with the following related materials and activities:

Topic: Facilitation and Administration
                      Reinforcement

Background: Workshop Preparation (pp. 36, 52)

Instructions

Description

This "session closer" encourages participants to apply the skills they learned in the workshop when they return to the workplace. This skill-application planning form is adapted with permission from *The Complete Training Course for Managers* by Irene E. McManus, Robert Paul McManus, and Bobette Hayes Williamson. The copyright holder, American Management Association, has granted permission to reproduce the material on condition that the credit line on the master appear on all reproduced copies.

Objectives

As a result of completing this plan, participants will be able to:

- Create a self-binding contract to apply skills learned in the workshop when they return to the job.

- Transfer learning from the workshop to the workplace.

Time

- 20 to 25 minutes.

Equipment

- None.

Materials

- One copy of the *Skill-Application Planner* for each participant (p. 210).

Procedure

1. Distribute the *Skill-Application Planner* and tell participants that it is important for them to begin using the skills they have learned at the workshop immediately when they return to their jobs. The Skill-Application Planner is designed to help them do just that. Ask them to select a skill that they will apply on the job, list steps they will take to apply the skill, state how they will measure their effectiveness in applying the skill, and then sign and date the form to make it a self-binding contract.
(2 minutes)

2. Participants complete the *Skill-Application Planner*.
(5 minutes)

3. Ask each participant to state the skill he or she plans to apply.
(10 minutes)

4. Congratulate participants on their action plans and express your confidence that they will implement the plans successfully.

Option

Have participants complete the *Skill-Application Planner* prior to the afternoon break. Collect the forms, have them photocopied, and return them to participants along with an envelope. Have the students address the envelope to themselves, enclose one copy of their *Skill-Application Planner*, and seal the envelope. Collect the envelopes and mail them to the students three months after the workshop as a reminder to apply the knowledge and skills gained during the workshop.

<u>HANDOUT</u>	## Skill-Application Planner
Directions	To help you apply the skills that you have learned in this course, fill out the worksheet below. When you sign and date the *Skill-Application Planner*, it becomes a self-binding contract.

1. **Course title:** (Example: Basic Supervision)

2. **Skill I will apply on the job:** (Example: Delegation)

3. **Steps I will take to apply the skill:**

    (Example: I will identify tasks to delegate by the end of this week. I will identify employees capable of performing the tasks by the end of this week.)

4. **How I will measure my effectiveness in applying the skill:**

    (Example: I will delegate four assignments within a week of this workshop. Completed work will meet agreed-upon performance standards.)

    Signature: _____

    Date: _____

Adapted with permission from *The Complete Training Course for Managers* by Irene E. McManus, Robert Paul McManus, and Bobette Hayes Williamson. Copyright ©1994 American Management Association, Watertown, MA.

Program Evaluation

REFERENCE CONTEXT

The Program Evaluation is used in conjunction with the following related materials and activities:

Topic: Facilitation and Administration

Background: Workshop Preparation (p. 52)

Scripts: One-Day Workshop, Module 5, (p. 82)

                         Half-Day Workshop, Module 4, (p. 110)

Instructions

Description   This evaluation is designed to be completed by participants at the close of the workshop.

Objectives   As a result of using this evaluation, the facilitator will:

- Learn the participants' degree of satisfaction with the workshop.

- Discover ways to improve the workshop.

Time   • 20 minutes.

Equipment   • None.

Materials   • Copies of the *Program Evaluation* for each participant (p. 212).

Procedure

1. Present a brief review of the workshop's key ideas. (5 minutes)

2. Ask participants for their feedback on the workshop. Distribute the evaluations and ask participants to complete them. Tell participants they are free to go when they have completed the evaluation, and designate a location where they can leave the completed evaluations.

HANDOUT

Program Evaluation

Course Title: _____

Trainer: _____ **Date:** _____

We welcome your opinions and comments. Please respond to each statement by circling the number of your choice, with 1 being a low grade and 5 being a high grade.

Course

		Low				High
1.	Objectives were clearly stated.	1	2	3	4	5
2.	Content will be useful on the job.	1	2	3	4	5
3.	Content was well organized.	1	2	3	4	5
4.	Examples, problems, case studies were helpful.	1	2	3	4	5
5.	Reading materials were easy to understand.	1	2	3	4	5
6.	Training media reinforced learning.	1	2	3	4	5
7.	Allowed enough time to achieve each objective.	1	2	3	4	5
8.	Training facilities met my needs.	1	2	3	4	5

Trainer

1.	Was always prepared.	1	2	3	4	5
2.	Had adequate subject knowledge.	1	2	3	4	5
3.	Communicated effectively.	1	2	3	4	5
4.	Presented content in an engaging manner.	1	2	3	4	5
5.	Encouraged trainees' participation.	1	2	3	4	5
6.	Was helpful with trainees' learning difficulties.	1	2	3	4	5
7.	Gave constructive feedback to trainees.	1	2	3	4	5
8.	Managed the course to my satisfaction.	1	2	3	4	5

Comments

(Begin comments below and continue on back of sheet.)

_____

_____

_____

_____

Adapted with permission from *The Complete Training Course for Managers* by Irene E. McManus, Robert Paul McManus, and Bobette Hayes Williamson. Copyright ©1994, American Management Association, Watertown, MA.

Chapter Ten:

Overhead Transparencies

In this chapter, you will find masters from which you can create overhead transparencies for use during your supervision workshops.

USING THE OVERHEAD TRANSPARENCIES

You may use the overhead transparencies in four ways:

- Key them into your word processing system "as is" or customize them to suit your specific needs.

- Photocopy the overhead transparency masters that you need from this book and use them "as is."

- Photocopy the masters on plain paper and distribute them as handouts.

- Create flipcharts by handlettering the content on sheets of 2′ x 3′ chart paper.

MANAGEMENT PROCESS

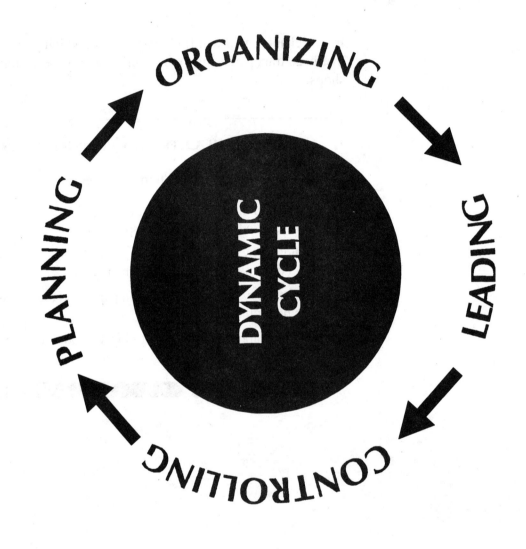

MANAGEMENT LEVELS

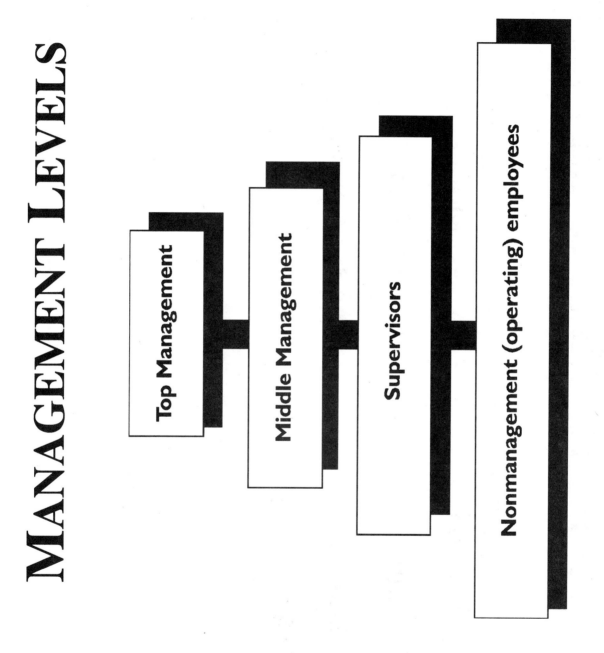

- Top Management
- Middle Management
- Supervisors
- Nonmanagement (operating) employees

SUPERVISORY RESPONSIBILITIES

- Production
- Quality
- Methods
- Safety

- Morale
- Costs
- Training

SUPERVISORY ROLES

- Coach
- Cheerleader
- Parent
- Hunter

- Team Captain
- Referee
- Gladiator
- Fortune Teller

SUPERVISORY JOB KNOWLEDGE

- Technical Knowledge

- Management of Resources

- Organizational Knowledge

- Industry Knowledge

MANAGEMENT SKILLS

- **Human Relations**

- **Technical**

- **Conceptual**

CHALLENGES FACING NEW SUPERVISORS

- Lack of Job Preparation

- Changes in Roles

- Changes in Relationships

- Changes in Perspective

- Lack of a Support System

DELEGATION PROCESS

1. Plan.

2. Organize.

3. Present project.

4. Involve employee.

5. Empower employee.

6. Track progress and provide support.

GIVING INSTRUCTIONS

- List each step.

- Show and tell.

- Watch body language.

- Check for understanding.

- Clarify misconceptions.

- Check on progress.

ROUND-ROBIN SKILL-PRACTICE

Skill Practice	Supervisor	Employee	Observer
Round 1	A	B	C
Round 2	B	C	A
Round 3	C	A	B

IMPLEMENTING A PLAN

1. Do homework.

2. Involve the team.

3. Write a plan.

4. Gain commitment.

5. Implement the plan.

6. Monitor progress.

7. Reward accomplishments.

Appendix:

Recommended Resources

This section is divided into two main parts:

RECOMMENDED RESOURCES

- Selected Bibliography

  The Selected Bibliography includes books and periodical articles on the topics covered in the background chapter.

- Resources for Training Professionals

  Resources for Training Professionals lists publishers of training materials in a section titled "Product Catalogs." By contacting these companies directly, the trainer can obtain product catalogs.

  Also mentioned under individual headings are pertinent films/videos, games/simulations, off-the-shelf programs, periodicals, and training sourcebooks.

The resources listed are presented for information purposes only. They do not imply any endorsement of the products or services by McGraw-Hill, Inc., American Society for Training and Development, or the author.

Selected Bibliography

Books

Bennis, Warren G., and Burt Nanus. *Leaders: The Strategies for Taking Charge*. New York: Harper and Row, 1985.

Describes four competencies of leaders: management of attention, management of meaning, management of trust, and management of self.

Bittel, Lester R. *The McGraw-Hill 36-Hour Management Course*. New York: McGraw-Hill, Inc., 1989.

This self-study course focuses on sixty concepts that are key to managerial success.

Bittel, Lester R., and John W. Newstrom. *What Every Supervisor Should Know*, Sixth Edition. New York: McGraw-Hill, 1990.

Written in a practical style that supervisors appreciate, this basic supervisory text is used in over one hundred two-year colleges and hundreds of businesses.

Boyd, Bradford B. *Management-Minded Supervision*. New York: McGraw-Hill, 1976.

Teaches first-line supervisors practical management skills via the case study method. Now out of print, this classic still may be available at some libraries.

Drucker, Peter F. *Post-Capitalist Society*. New York: HarperBusiness, 1993.

Analyzes the trends affecting society, economics, business, and politics in the post-capitalist society.

Hammer, Michael, and James Champy. *Reengineering the Corporation: A Manifesto for Business Revolution*. New York: HarperBusiness, 1993.

Shows how corporations redesign processes, cultures, and structures for maximum performance.

Harris, Philip R. *High Performance Leadership: Strategies for Maximum Productivity*. Glenview, IL: Scott, Foresman and Company, 1989.

Explains how to create a high-performance work environment, motivate and teach employees, and cope with organizational change.

Harris, Philip R. *Management in Transition.* San Francisco: Jossey-Bass Publishers, 1985.

Examines how new technologies are impacting on work, reshaping its nature and scope, and requiring new forms of management adaptation.

Koonz, Harold, and Heinz Weihrich. *Essentials of Management,* Fifth Edition. New York: McGraw-Hill, 1990.

Covers the theory and practice of management. A chapter on international management discusses managerial practices in Asian countries and in Europe.

Kouzes, James M. and Barry Z. Posner. *The Leadership Challenge: How To Get Extraordinary Things Done in Organizations.* San Francisco: Jossey-Bass Publishers, 1987.

Describes five leadership practices and ten specific behaviors that can be applied by managers at all levels.

Osborne, David, and Ted Gaebler. *Reinventing Government: How the Entrepreneurial Spirit is Transforming the Public Sector.* New York: Plume, 1993.

Describes how enterprising public officials have helped their organizations to become more efficient, competitive, results oriented, and forward thinking.

Peters, Tom. *Liberation Management: Necessary Disorganization for the Nanosecond Nineties.* New York: Alfred A. Knopf, 1992.

In the new Information Age economy, enterprises are undergoing major shifts in the way they are organized. Most work will be brainwork, done in semipermanent networks of small project-oriented teams.

Toffler, Alvin. *Powershift: Knowledge, Wealth, and Violence at the Edge of the 21st Century.* New York: Bantam Books, 1990.

Focuses on a new power system in which knowledge is the key raw material for wealth creation. Part Four, "Power in the Flex-Firm," is particularly relevant.

Weiss, W. H. *Supervisor's Standard Reference Handbook* (Second Edition). Englewood Cliffs, NJ: Prentice-Hall, Inc., 1988.

Provides practical techniques for solving everyday supervisory problems.

Periodicals

Bridges, William. "The End of the Job." *Fortune*, September 19, 1994, pp. 62-74.

> The job as a way of organizing work has outlived its usefulness. Explores the impact of this phenomenon on organizations, managers, and nonmanagerial employees, and describes how some "post-job" organizations are responding.

Byrne, John A., Wendy Zellner, and Scott Ticer. "Caught in the Middle." *Business Week*, September 12, 1988, pp. 80-88.

> Reviews the effects of restructuring on middle managers.

Castro, Janice. "Disposable Workers." *Time*, March 29, 1993, pp. 43-47.

> The move toward a disposable workforce is fundamentally changing the relationship between Americans and their jobs.

Deutschman, Alan. "Pioneers of the New Balance." *Fortune*, May 20, 1991, pp. 60-68.

> Presents a positive picture of how flexible work schedules benefit both employers and employees.

"Employers Scramble To Retain 'Plateaued' Workers." *The Wall Street Journal*, February 19, 1991, p. 1.

> Describes steps employees are taking to reward and retain plateaued workers.

Fierman, Jaclyn. "The Contingency Work Force." *Fortune*, January 24, 1994, pp. 30-36.

> Examines the trend toward replacing full-time permanent employees with contingent workers.

Garland, Susan, Laura Zinn, Christopher Power, Maria Shao, and Julia Flynn Siler. "Those Aging Boomers." *Business Week*, May 20, 1991, pp. 106-110.

> Focuses on boomers who realize it will be tough to reach the level of affluence their parents enjoyed.

Hequet, Marc. "How Telecommuting Transforms Work." *Training*, November 1994, pp. 56-61.

> Discusses pros and cons of telecommuting.

Hymowitz, Carol. "When Firms Cut Out Middle Managers. Those at Top and Bottom Often Suffer." *The Wall Street Journal*, April 5, 1990, p. B1.

Reviews adjustments middle managers must make in downsized organizations. Discusses the impact of the middle managers' changed roles and functions on first-line supervisors and rank-and-file employees.

Katz, Robert L. "Skills of an Effective Administrator." *Harvard Business Review*, September-October 1974, p. 94.

Landmark article that classifies essential skills of managers into three categories: technical, human, and conceptual. Most management texts use Katz' classifications.

Koretz, Gene. "Downward Mobility Is Stalking The Baby Boomers." *Business Week*, January 28, 1991, p. 22.

Baby boomers own fewer assets than their parents did at similar points in their lives.

Morrow, Lance. "The Temping of America." *Time*, March 29, 1993, pp. 40-41.

America has entered the age of the just-in-time workforce. Companies are portable and workers are throwaways.

Nulty, Peter. "How Managers Will Manage." *Fortune*, February 2, 1987, pp. 47-50.

Managing used to mean getting things done through others. Now it means getting value added. Value-added managers tangibly improve products or profits.

Rigdon, Joan E. "Using Lateral Moves to Spur Employees." *The Wall Street Journal*, May 26, 1992, p. B1.

Describes how employers encourage employees to take lateral moves and nontraditional career paths.

Sherman, Stratford. "A Brave New Darwinian Workplace." *Fortune*, January 25, 1993, pp. 50-56.

Examines the new relationship that is evolving between employer and employee as the forces of technology and economics destroy the organizational hierarchy.

Stewart, Thomas A. "Managing in a Wired Company." *Fortune*, July 11, 1994, pp. 44-56.

Describes how organizations change after the implementation of network technology.

Resources for Training Professionals

Product catalogs

The following are sources for training and development materials. Phone or write to obtain product catalogs.

American Management Association, 135 West 50th Street, New York, NY 10020. Phone: 800-262-9699.

American Society for Training and Development, 1640 King Street, Alexandria, VA 22313. Phone: 800-628-2783, 703-683-8100.

Aviat, 555 Briarwood Circle, Suite 140, Ann Arbor, MI 48108. Phone: 800-421-5323, 313-663-2386.

Blanchard Training and Development, Inc., 125 State Place, Escondido, CA 92029. Phone: 800-728-6000.

CRM Films, 2215 Faraday Avenue, Carlsbad, CA 92008-7295. Phone: 800-421-0833.

Career Track Publications, MS 20-13, P.O. Box 18778, 3085 Center Green Drive, Boulder, CO 80308-1778. Phone: 800-334-1018, 303-442-0392.

Crisp Publications, 1200 Hamilton Court, Menlo Park, CA 94025. Phone: 800-442-7477, 415-323-6100.

Films Incorporated PMI, 5547 N. Ravenswood Avenue, Chicago, IL 60640. Phone: 800-323-4222, 312-878-2600.

HRD Press, 22 Amherst Road, Amherst, MA 01002. Phone: 800-822-2801, 413-253-3488.

Human Synergistics International, 39819 Plymouth Road, C-8020, Plymouth, MI 48170. Phone: 800-622-7584, 313-459-1030.

Lakewood Publications, 50 South Ninth Street, The Lakewood Building, Minneapolis, MN 55402. Phone: 800-707-7769, 612-333-0471.

Nightingale-Conant Corporation, 7300 N. Lehigh Avenue, Niles, IL 60714. Phone: 800-323-5552, 708-647-0300.

Pfeiffer & Company, 2780 Circleport Drive, Erlanger, KY 41018. Phone: 800-274-4434, 606-647-3030.

Talico Incorporated, 2320 South Third Street, #5, Jacksonville Beach, FL 32250. Phone: 904-241-1721.

Vital Learning, 444 Regency Parkway Drive, Suite 201, Omaha, NE 68114. Phone: 800-243-5858, 402-391-2542.

Films/Videos

Change

New Workplace. Quality Media Resources. Available through CRM Films, 2215 Faraday Avenue, Carlsbad, CA 92008-7295. Phone: 800-421-0833.

Stimulates discussion about changing relationships between employees and employers. Program 1 is "Making the Change" and Program 2 is "Leading the Change." Running time: 23 minutes per program.

Controlling

Correct Way of Correcting. Roundtable/CRM Films, 2215 Faraday Avenue, Carlsbad, CA 92008-7295. Phone: 800-421-0833.

Set in the Old West, this video features Cookie the Cook who demonstrates six proven methods for correcting without destroying morale. Running time: 24 minutes.

Discipline Without Punishment (Revised Version). CRM Films, 2215 Faraday Avenue, Carlsbad, CA 92008-7295. Phone: 800-421-0833.

Work-related scenarios help managers use positive discipline techniques to instill self-discipline in employees. Running time: 20 minutes.

Leading

Innovation. American Management Association, Nine Galen Street, P.O. Box 9119, Watertown, MA 02272. Phone: 800-225-3215.

Video Number 1, "Inspiring Innovation," shows managers how to encourage and champion innovation. Running time: 24 minutes. Video Number 2, "Creating Innovations," illustrates key components of the innovation process. Running time: 20 minutes.

Leadership and the One Minute Manager. Video Publishing House Inc. Available from Films Incorporated PMI, 5547 N. Ravenswood Avenue, Chicago, IL 60640. Phone: 800-323-4222, 312-878-2600.

In this classic video, Ken Blanchard explains how managers can develop competence and commitment in employees. Running time: 80 minutes.

Rewards of Rewarding. Roundtable/CRM Films, 2215 Faraday Avenue, Carlsbad, CA 92008-7295. Phone: 800-421-0833.

Set in the Old West, Cookie the Cook teaches the ranch owner and foreman that acknowledging good performance motivates employees to aspire to consistently high standards. Running time: 24 minutes.

The Leadership Challenge. CRM Films, 2215 Faraday Avenue, Carlsbad, CA 92008-7295. Phone: 800-421-0833.

Based on the best-selling book of the same title. Authors James Kouzes and Barry Posner cover five leadership practices that anyone can apply. Each principle is illustrated with an actual case example. Running time: 26 minutes.

Planning and organizing

A Perfectly Normal Day. Available from Films Incorporated PMI, 5547 N. Ravenswood Avenue, Chicago, IL 60640. Phone: 800-323-4222, 312-878-2600.

Describes time management techniques that help to control and reduce daily interruptions and crises. Running time: 27 minutes.

The Time of Your Life. Available from Films Incorporated PMI, 5547 N. Ravenswood Avenue, Chicago, IL 60640. Phone: 800-323-4222, 312-878-2600.

Based on Alan Lakein's book of the same title. Explains the fundamentals of time management by emphasizing listing goals, setting priorities, handling each piece of paper only once, and eliminating procrastination. Suggests more than sixty time-saving tips. Running time: 27 minutes.

The Unorganized Manager. Video Arts Productions, 8614 W. Catalpa Avenue, Chicago, IL 60656. Phone: 800-553-0091, 312-693-9966.

Four-part series featuring John Cleese demonstrates how to organize work, set priorities, schedule tasks, and organize others. Running time: between 20 and 29 minutes per part.

Where Does the Time Go? American Management Association, Nine Galen Street, P.O. Box 9119, Watertown, MA 02272. Phone: 800-225-3215.

Shows how to deal with changing priorities, interruptions, and crises, as well as how to create a time management blueprint. Describes four-quadrant time management. Running time: 12 minutes.

Supervision

After All, You're the Supervisor. Roundtable/CRM Films, 2215 Faraday Avenue, Carlsbad, CA 92008-7295. Phone: 800-421-0833.

Follows a new supervisor as he performs his daily responsibilities. Lists seventeen keys to supervisory success. The supervisor shares some of his early mistakes, while modeling effective behaviors. Running time: 20 minutes.

Focusing on the Human Side. Bureau of Business Practice. Available from American Management Association, Nine Galen Street, P.O. Box 9119, Watertown, MA 02272. Phone: 800-225-3215.

Shows five behaviors that help supervisors to manage effectively. Stresses tailoring leadership style to fit the situation. Running time: 27 minutes.

Learning to Think Like a Manager. CRM Films, 2215 Faraday Avenue, Carlsbad, CA 92008-7295. Phone: 800-421-0833.

Illustrates three common mistakes that new supervisors make, and shows how three recently-promoted supervisors make the transition from operating employees to managers. Filmed in an office setting. Running time: 25 minutes.

The New Supervisor. American Management Association, Nine Galen Street, P.O. Box 9119, Watertown, MA 02272. Phone: 800-225-3215.

Covers management of work, management of others, and management of self. Martin Broadwell, author of the text *The New Supervisor*, is the on-camera subject matter expert. Running time: 64 minutes, with stop points for participant skill practice.

Games/Simulations

Nicholls, Ian. *50 Activities for Developing Supervisory Skills.* HRD Press, Amherst, MA, 1993.

The activities in the manual are designed to help trainees learn for themselves in a participative way. Topics include planning, organizing, directing, problem solving, decision making, motivation, communication, and running meetings.

Scannell, Edward E., and John W. Newstrom. *The Complete Games Trainers Play: Experiential Learning Exercises.* New York: McGraw-Hill, Inc., 1994.

Contains 287 ready-to-use training games, plus a trainer's resource kit that is chock full of information and checklists to help the user administer, design, and deliver successful training programs.

Off-the-Shelf Programs

Leading

Williamson, Bobette Hayes, Robert Paul McManus, and Irene E. McManus. *Creating a Competitive Advantage Through Innovation*. Watertown, MA: American Management Association, 1992.

A self-study course that covers the role of the innovator; how enterprises can design strategies, structures, and practices to foster innovation; discovering ideas for new ventures; enrolling others in the vision, and turning vision into reality.

Planning

Williamson, Bobette Hayes, Robert P. McManus, and Irene E. McManus. *Performance Excellence Planning: A Workshop in Goal Setting and Career Development*. Vital Learning, Omaha, NE, 1989. Address: Vital Learning, 444 Regency Parkway Drive, Suite 201, Omaha, NE 68114. Phone: 800-243-5858.

Teaches a five-step planning process for achieving professional excellence.

Supervision

Engler, David. *Supervision Series*. Vital Learning, Omaha, NE, 1986. Address: Vital Learning, 444 Regency Parkway Drive, Suite 201, Omaha, NE 68114. Phone: 800-243-5858.

Seventeen-module series that emphasizes behavior modeling and skill practice. Office and industrial versions.

Train-the-Trainer

McManus, Irene E., Robert P. McManus, and Bobette Hayes Williamson. *The Complete Training Course for Managers*. American Management Association, 135 West 50th Street, New York, NY 10020. Phone: 800-262-9699.

A self-study course for trainers and supervisors. Presents a four-phase training model which includes needs assessment, instructional design, course delivery, and evaluation.

Periodicals

Training and Development Journal. American Society for Training and Development, Box 1443, 1630 Duke Street, Alexandria, VA 22313. Phone: 703-683-8100.

Monthly journal covers current issues of interest to human resource development professionals. Also contains practical, how-to articles.

Training: The Human Side of Business. Lakewood Publications, Inc., 50 S. Ninth St., Minneapolis, MN 55402. Phone: 612-333-0471.

Monthly magazine devoted to training issues and skills. Each year the October issue contains an in-depth review of the training industry.

Training Sourcebooks

The ASTD Trainer's Sourcebooks are a series of reproducible toolkits that allow trainers to create their own workshops. Like this *Supervision Sourcebook*, the other volumes in the series contain reproducible handouts and overhead transparency masters, activities, instruments, surveys, and fully scripted training designs. Volumes in the series cover such topics as coaching, customer service, diversity, leadership, project management, quality, sales, strategic planning, supervision, and teams.

Index

About the Author

Bobette Hayes Williamson is a seminar leader, instructional designer, and business writer with over twenty years of experience helping supervisors, teams, and individuals develop strong management skills to apply in the changing business world. Williamson is an instructor for both the San Diego (California) Community College District Employment Training Institute, where she teaches supervision, and for University of California San Diego Extension, Department of Business and Management, where she teaches "Interpersonal Communication and Professional Development."

Williamson is co-author of *The Complete Training Course for Managers* (1993) and *Creating A Competitive Advantage Through Innovation* (1992), both American Management Association self-study courses. Williamson is also co-author of *Performance Excellence Planning: A Goal Setting and Career Development Workshop* (Vital Learning, 1989). She is author or co-author of 19 leader's guides for CRM training films. She was a member of the team that wrote McGraw-Hill Training Systems' 17-module *SUPERVISION* series.

In addition to maintaining a consulting and training practice since 1978, Williamson served as a communications specialist at United Way of San Diego County for three years. Responsibilities included coordinating a speakers and tours bureau, marketing, media relations, and in-house training. She also worked for eleven years in a civilian capacity at a U.S. Navy research center in San Diego. Positions held were public information specialist, personnel management specialist, and equal opportunity specialist.

Williamson is past president of both the San Diego Chapter of the American Society for Training and Development (ASTD) and the San Diego Chapter of the International Association of Business Communicators (IABC). She has received San Diego ASTD's Spotlight Award, which is presented annually to a member who gains national or international recognition for writing. She is also a member of the Central Oregon Speakers Association.

Williamson holds B.A. and M.A. degrees from University of California, Berkeley. She took graduate studies in education at San Jose State University. She holds a lifetime California community college teaching credential.

"KNOWLEDGE AND HUMAN POWER ARE SYNONYMOUS"

*K*nowledge generates human performance. It doesn't take a famous quote or the picture of a tree to know that. But full potential requires the proper elements. Your professional growth can thrive, as a member of the American Society for Training and Development.

As an ASTD member you will get:

Information on the forefront of practice and technology

Access to colleagues around the world for idea-sharing

Opportunity to contribute to the advancement of your profession

through...international conferences and expositions...best practices...electronic resources and networking...benchmarking publications...personalized research assistance...and much more.

Join ASTD now...and become part of a worldwide association of nearly 58,000 leaders in the field of workplace learning and performance.

Call 703.683.8100. Or fax 703.683.1523
Mention Priority Code: MH5A
TDD: 703.683.4323

 ASTD
AMERICAN SOCIETY
FOR TRAINING AND
DEVELOPMENT

Delivering Performance in a Changing World